Favorite Brand Name

4 INGREDIENT COOKBOOK

Fast & Easy Recipes

Publications International, Ltd.
Favorite Brand Name Recipes at www.fbnr.com

Copyright © 2001 Publications International, Ltd.
All rights reserved. This publication may not be reproduced or quoted in whole or in part by any means whatsoever without written permission from:

Louis Weber, CEO
Publications International, Ltd.
7373 North Cicero Avenue
Lincolnwood, IL 60712

Permission is never granted for commercial purposes.

All recipes and photographs that contain specific brand names are copyrighted by those companies and/or associations, unless otherwise specified. All photographs *except* those on pages 14, 43, 47, 67, 73, 93, 95, 96, 98, 108, 116, 125, 127, 179, 254, 261, 275, 289, 293, 297, 301, 313, 317, 323, 338, 353, 355, 357, 359 and 365 copyright © Publications International, Ltd.

BREYERS® is a registered trademark of Unilever, N.V., used under license.

DOLE® is a registered trademark of Dole Food Company, Inc.

LOUIS RICH® is a registered trademark of Oscar Mayer Foods Corporation.

™/© M&M's, M and the M&M's Characters are trademarks of Mars, Incorporated.
© Mars, Inc. 2001.

Albers, Libby's, Nestlé and Toll House are registered trademarks of Nestlé.

TACO BELL® and HOME ORIGINALS® are trademarks owned and licensed by Taco Bell Corp.

Some of the products listed in this publication may be in limited distribution.

Photography on pages 9, 12, 19, 29, 55, 61, 139, 176, 186, 187, 192, 299, 303, 307 and 321 by
Scott Payne Studios, Inc., Chicago.

Pictured on the front cover *(left to right):* Peachy Pork Roast *(page 60),* Shrimp & Asparagus Fettucine *(page 159)* and Black Forest Torte *(page 316).*
Pictured on the back cover *(left to right):* Bandito Buffalo Wings *(page 8),* Sweet & Sour Pork *(page 64)* and Jalapeño Pepper Steak *(page 54).*

ISBN: 0-7853-5161-2

Library of Congress Catalog Card Number: 00-110379

Manufactured in China.

8 7 6 5 4 3 2 1

Microwave Cooking: Microwave ovens vary in wattage. Use the cooking times as guidelines and check for doneness before adding more time.

Preparation/Cooking Times: Preparation times are based on the approximate amount of time required to assemble the recipe before cooking, baking, chilling or serving. These times include preparation steps such as measuring, chopping and mixing. The fact that some preparations and cooking can be done simultaneously is taken into account. Preparation of optional ingredients and serving suggestions is not included.

Contents

Introduction

Welcome to simple, fast cooking without the fuss. With the 4 Ingredient Cookbook, you can now create tasty, exciting dishes without spending hours at the store gathering a long list of ingredients—or in the kitchen following complex recipe instructions. You can easily create most of these dishes, many of which are whole meals, in less time than it takes to go for carry-out food. And, preparing a home-cooked meal—especially one that is easy for the kids to help create—is a great way to get the family together and avoid the all-too-common tendency to order out.

The 4 *Ingredient Cookbook* is full of easy-to-follow recipes, many with four ingredients or less. This number excludes ingredients common to many recipes and found in most kitchens: water, nonstick cooking spray, salt and pepper. Also not counted are implements such as skewers and racks, and ingredients labeled as "optional" or "for garnish."

Cooking with these recipes can save you a lot of time. Get the most out of this book by planning your meals in advance. Be sure to read through any recipes you're making before you go shopping, to be certain you buy all the needed ingredients.

Many recipes can be prepared so quickly that you can put together appetizers, side dishes or desserts while a main course is cooking. Some quick-assemble dishes take only a few minutes to prepare but require a longer time in the oven or slow cooker; others need time to marinate. Spend the extra time exercising, doing errands or relaxing with the family. That's what the 4 *Ingredient Cookbook* is designed to do: free you up to do other things!

Use the helpful tips in the sidebars or within the recipes to streamline your preparation and cooking processes.

 "Quick Tips" tell you how to save time in the supermarket and the kitchen

 "Smart Tips" offer suggestions on cooking or ingredients that can help you to make a better meal

 "Serving Tips" give you ideas on how to simplify and enhance your meal presentation

Appetizers & Drinks

Start off a special meal with a quick and easy appetizer, or add an accompanying drink to liven things up. It will heighten expectations for the main dish…and everyone will remember an event, not just a meal.

Right:
V8® Bloody Mary Mocktail (recipe on page 32) and Pace® Chili con Queso Bites (recipe on page 20)

Cheese Straws

¹/₂ cup (1 stick) butter, softened
¹/₈ teaspoon salt
    Dash ground red pepper
1 pound sharp Cheddar cheese, shredded, at room temperature
2 cups self-rising flour

Heat oven to 350°F. In mixer bowl, beat butter, salt and pepper until creamy. Add cheese; mix well. Gradually add flour, mixing until dough begins to form a ball. Form dough into ball with hands.

Fit cookie press with small star plate; fill with dough according to manufacturer's directions. Press dough onto cookie sheets in 3-inch-long strips. Bake 12 minutes or until lightly browned. Cool completely on wire rack. Store tightly covered.

Makes about 10 dozen

Right: *Cheese Straws*

Bandito Buffalo Wings

1 package (1 ¹/₄ ounces) ORTEGA® Taco Seasoning Mix
1 pound (about 12) chicken wings
    ORTEGA® Thick & Chunky Salsa, hot, medium or mild

PLACE taco seasoning mix in large resealable plastic food-storage bag. Add chicken wings, a few at a time; shake well to coat. Repeat until all wings have been coated. Place wings on lightly greased baking pan.

BAKE in preheated 375°F oven for 35 to 40 minutes or until no longer pink near bone. Serve with salsa for dipping.

Makes 6 servings

Above:
Bandito Buffalo Wings

Devilish Eggs

Prep Time: *40 minutes*   **Chill Time:** *30 minutes*

12 hard-cooked eggs, cut in half
 6 tablespoons low-fat mayonnaise
 2 tablespoons *French's®* Mustard (any flavor)
¼ teaspoon salt
⅛ teaspoon ground red pepper

1. Remove yolk from egg whites using teaspoon. Press yolks through sieve with back of spoon or mash with fork in medium bowl. Stir in mayonnaise, mustard, salt and red pepper; mix well.

2. Spoon or pipe yolk mixture into egg whites. Arrange on serving platter. Garnish, if desired. Cover; chill in refrigerator until ready to serve.   *Makes 12 servings*

Zesty Variations: Stir in one of the following: 2 tablespoons minced red onion plus 1 tablespoon horseradish; 2 tablespoons pickle relish plus 1 tablespoon minced fresh dill; 2 tablespoons each minced onion and celery plus 1 tablespoon minced fresh dill; or ¼ cup (1 ounce) shredded Cheddar cheese plus ½ teaspoon *French's®* Worcestershire Sauce.

Cocktail Bites

1 ¼ cups red currant jelly or cranberry sauce
1 ¼ cups ketchup
 2 pounds HILLSHIRE FARM® Lit'l Smokies

Heat jelly and ketchup in small saucepan over medium heat *or* microwave, uncovered, at HIGH 1 to 2 minutes just until mixture blends smoothly. Add Lit'l Smokies; cook until links are hot. Serve with frilled toothpicks.

Makes about 100 hors d'oeuvres

Right:
Devilish Eggs

Hot Artichoke Dip

1 cup MIRACLE WHIP® Salad Dressing or KRAFT® Real Mayonnaise
1 cup (4 ounces) KRAFT® 100% Grated Parmesan Cheese
1 (14-ounce) can artichoke hearts, drained, chopped

• Heat oven to 350°F.

• Mix all ingredients; spoon into 9-inch pie plate or 2-cup casserole.

• Bake 20 minutes or until lightly browned. Garnish as desired. Serve with tortilla chips, crackers or party rye bread slices.   *Makes about 2 cups*

Below:
Guacamole

Guacamole

2 large avocados, peeled and pitted
¼ cup finely chopped tomato
2 tablespoons lime juice or lemon juice
2 tablespoons grated onion with juice
½ teaspoon salt
¼ teaspoon hot pepper sauce
Black pepper

Place avocados in medium bowl; mash coarsely with fork. Stir in tomato, lime juice, onion, salt and pepper sauce; mix well. Add black pepper to taste. Spoon into serving container. Serve immediately or cover and refrigerate up to 2 hours. Garnish with additional chopped tomatoes, if desired.   *Makes 2 cups*

Baked Mozzarella Sticks

Butter-flavored nonstick cooking spray
12 ounces (2 blocks) ALPINE LACE® Fat Free Pasteurized Process Skim
Milk Cheese Product—For Mozzarella Lovers
½ cup egg substitute *or* **2 large eggs**
1 cup Italian seasoned dry bread crumbs
¼ cup minced fresh parsley

1. Preheat the oven to 400°F. Spray 2 large baking sheets with the cooking spray.

2. Cut each block of cheese in half crosswise, then each half lengthwise into 3 equal sticks (about 3×¾ inches), making a total of 12 sticks.

3. In a medium-size bowl, whisk the egg substitute (or the whole eggs) until frothy. On a plate, toss the bread crumbs with the parsley.

4. Dip each cheese stick first into the egg substitute, then roll in the bread crumbs, pressing them slightly as you go. Arrange the cheese in a single layer on the baking sheets.

5. Spray the sticks lightly with the cooking spray. Bake for 10 minutes or until golden brown and crispy.   *Makes 12 cheese sticks*

BelGioioso® Fontina Melt

1 loaf Italian or French bread
2 fresh tomatoes, cubed
Basil leaves, julienned
BELGIOIOSO® Fontina Cheese, sliced

Cut bread lengthwise into halves. Top each half with tomatoes and sprinkle with basil. Top with BelGioioso Fontina Cheese. Place in oven at 350°F for 10 to 12 minutes or until cheese is golden brown.   *Makes 6 to 8 servings*

Cheddar Tomato Bacon Toasts

Prep Time: 10 *minutes*   **Cook Time:** 10 *minutes*

1 jar (16 ounces) RAGÚ® Cheese Creations!® Double Cheddar Sauce
1 medium tomato, chopped
5 slices bacon, crisp-cooked and crumbled (about ⅓ cup)
2 loaves Italian bread (each about 16 inches long), each cut into 16 slices

1. Preheat oven to 350°F. In medium bowl, combine Ragú Cheese Creations! Sauce, tomato and bacon.

2. On baking sheet, arrange bread slices. Evenly top with sauce mixture.

3. Bake 10 minutes or until sauce mixture is bubbling. Serve hot.

Makes 16 servings

Right:
*Cheddar Tomato
Bacon Toasts*

Philadelphia® Cranberry Orange Spread

Prep Time: 5 *minutes*

1 package (8 ounces) PHILADELPHIA® Cream Cheese, softened
½ cup cranberry orange sauce
3 tablespoons chopped pecans, toasted

SPREAD cream cheese on serving plate.

TOP with sauce; sprinkle with pecans. Serve with crackers.   *Makes 10 servings*

Above:
*Philadelphia®
Cranberry Orange
Spread*

Campbell's® Asparagus & Ham Potato Topper

Prep and Cook Time: *10 minutes*

4 hot baked potatoes, split
1 cup diced cooked ham
1 can (10¾ ounces) CAMPBELL'S® Condensed Cream of Asparagus Soup
    Shredded Cheddar *or* Swiss cheese (optional)

1. Place hot baked potatoes on microwave-safe plate. Carefully fluff up potatoes with fork.

2. Top each potato with ham. Stir soup in can until smooth. Spoon soup over potatoes. Top with cheese, if desired. Microwave on HIGH 4 minutes or until hot.

Makes 4 servings

Quick Tip

For evenly cooked potatoes, be sure to choose potatoes that are about the same size.

Danish Blue Truffles

1 cup California walnut pieces
8 ounces Danish Blue Castello cheese,* chilled

*If Danish Blue Castello cheese is unavailable, substitute Danish Blue cheese. Blend with milk or cream, 1 tablespoon at a time, until blue cheese mixture becomes the consistency of cream cheese.

Spread walnuts in shallow baking pan. Bake in 350°F oven, stirring occasionally, 12 to 15 minutes or until toasted and golden. Cool walnuts, then chop.

Beat cheese until smooth with wooden spoon. Divide into 18 pieces; roll each piece into a ball. Roll each ball in walnuts to coat. Serve chilled.

Makes 1½ dozen appetizers

Favorite recipe from **Walnut Marketing Board**

Sugar 'n' Spice Nuts

4 cups assorted salted mixed nuts
2 tablespoons I CAN'T BELIEVE IT'S NOT BUTTER!® Spread, melted
3 tablespoons sugar
1 to 2 teaspoons ground red pepper
2 teaspoons dried coriander (optional)

Preheat oven to 300°F.

In large bowl, combine mixed nuts and I Can't Believe It's Not Butter! Spread; set aside.

In small bowl, blend remaining ingredients; stir into nut mixture. On ungreased baking sheet, evenly spread nut mixture.

Bake, stirring occasionally, 40 minutes or until nuts are golden.

Makes 4 cups nuts

Bourbon Dogs

2 cups ketchup
¾ cup bourbon
½ cup dark brown sugar
1 tablespoon grated onion
1 pound HILLSHIRE FARM® Lit'l Smokies

Combine ketchup, bourbon, brown sugar and onion in medium saucepan. Stir in Lit'l Smokies; simmer over low heat or bake in 300°F oven 1 hour.* Serve hot.

Makes about 50 hors d'oeuvres

*If mixture becomes too thick, thin with additional bourbon or water.

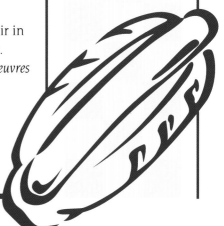

Shrimp and Snow Pea Appetizers with Currant Mustard Sauce

6 ounces fresh snow peas (about 36)
1 ½ pounds medium shrimp, peeled, deveined and cooked
¾ cup SMUCKER'S® Currant Jelly
¼ cup Dijon mustard

Blanch snow peas in boiling salted water for 45 seconds. Immediately drain and run under cold water.

Wrap 1 blanched pea pod around each shrimp and secure with toothpick.

Combine jelly and mustard; beat with a fork or wire whisk until smooth. (Jelly will dissolve in about 5 minutes.) Serve sauce with appetizers.   *Makes 36 appetizers*

Crabmeat Spread
Prep Time: *5 minutes*

1 package (8 ounces) light cream cheese, softened
¼ cup cocktail sauce
1 package (8 ounces) imitation crabmeat

Spread cream cheese evenly on serving plate. Pour cocktail sauce over cream cheese; top with imitation crabmeat.

Serve with cocktail rye bread or assorted crackers.   *Makes 12 servings*

Right:
Shrimp and Snow Pea Appetizers with Currant Mustard Sauce

Tortellini Kabobs with Pesto Ranch Dip
Prep and Cook Time: 30 *minutes*

½ bag (16 ounces) frozen tortellini
1¼ cups ranch salad dressing
½ cup grated Parmesan cheese
3 cloves garlic, minced
2 teaspoons dried basil leaves

1. Cook tortellini according to package directions. Rinse and drain under cold water. Thread tortellini onto bamboo skewers, 2 tortellini per skewer.

2. Combine salad dressing, cheese, garlic and basil in small bowl. Serve tortellini kabobs with dip.   *Makes 6 to 8 servings*

Right:
Tortellini Kabobs with Pesto Ranch Dip

Pace® Chili con Queso Bites
Prep Time: 10 *minutes*   **Cook Time:** 10 *minutes*

4 eggs
½ cup PACE® Picante Sauce *or* Thick & Chunky Salsa
¼ cup all-purpose flour
2 teaspoons chili powder
1½ cups shredded Cheddar cheese (6 ounces)
1 green onion, chopped (about 2 tablespoons)

1. Preheat oven to 400°F. Grease 24 (3-inch) muffin-pan cups. Set aside.

2. In medium bowl mix eggs, picante sauce, flour and chili powder. Stir in cheese and onion.

3. Spoon about **1 *tablespoon*** cheese mixture into each cup. Bake 10 minutes or until golden brown. Serve warm or at room temperature with sour cream and additional picante sauce, if desired.   *Makes 24 appetizers*

Tip: Baked appetizers may be frozen. To reheat, bake frozen appetizers at 350°F. for 10 minutes or until hot.

Above:
Pace® Chili con Queso Bites

Smoked Salmon Appetizers

¼ cup reduced-fat or fat-free cream cheese, softened
1 tablespoon chopped fresh dill *or* 1 teaspoon dried dill weed
⅛ teaspoon ground red pepper
4 ounces thinly sliced smoked salmon or lox
24 melba toast rounds or other low-fat crackers

1. Combine cream cheese, dill and pepper in small bowl; stir to blend. Spread evenly over each slice of salmon. Roll up salmon slices jelly-roll fashion. Place on plate; cover with plastic wrap. Chill at least 1 hour or up to 4 hours before serving.

2. Using a sharp knife, cut salmon rolls crosswise into ¾-inch pieces. Place pieces, cut sides down, on serving plate. Garnish each salmon roll with dill sprig, if desired. Serve cold or at room temperature with melba rounds.

Makes about 2 dozen appetizers

Pretzels with a Chicken Twist

Prep Time: *15 minutes*

2 packages BUTTERBALL® Chicken Breast Tenders, halved lengthwise
½ cup prepared honey mustard
2 cups crushed pretzels

Preheat oven to 400°F. Pour honey mustard into shallow bowl. Add chicken tenders and turn to coat. Discard any remaining honey mustard. Roll coated chicken in crushed pretzels. Place on baking sheet sprayed with nonstick cooking spray. Bake 5 to 8 minutes or until chicken is no longer pink in center. Serve with extra honey mustard for dipping.

Makes 32 appetizers

Right:
*Smoked Salmon
Appetizers*

Can't Get Enough Chicken Wings

18 chicken wings (about 3 pounds)
 1 envelope LIPTON® RECIPE SECRETS® Savory Herb with Garlic
     Soup Mix
½ cup water
 2 to 3 tablespoons hot pepper sauce* (optional)
 2 tablespoons margarine or butter

*Use more or less hot pepper sauce as desired.

1. Cut tips off chicken wings (save tips for soup). Cut chicken wings in half at joint. Deep fry, bake or broil until golden brown and crunchy.

2. Meanwhile, in small saucepan, combine soup mix, water and hot pepper sauce. Cook over low heat, stirring occasionally, 2 minutes or until thickened. Remove from heat and stir in margarine.

3. In large bowl, toss cooked chicken wings with hot soup mixture until evenly coated. Serve, if desired, over greens with cut-up celery.   *Makes 36 appetizers*

Smart Tip

To make your own chicken stock, simmer chicken wing tips with water, onion, celery and bay leaf for 1 to 2 hours. Strain, skim off fat, and freeze in containers for later use.

Right:
Can't Get Enough Chicken Wings

Chicken Nuggets Parmigiana
Prep Time: 5 minutes   **Cook Time:** 30 minutes

1 jar (26 to 28 ounces) RAGÚ® Old World Style® Pasta Sauce
1 package (12 ounces) refrigerated or frozen fully-cooked chicken
    nuggets (about 18 nuggets)
2 cups shredded mozzarella cheese (about 8 ounces)
1 tablespoon grated Parmesan cheese

1. Preheat oven to 375°F. In 13×9-inch baking dish, evenly spread 1½ cups Ragú Pasta Sauce. Arrange chicken nuggets in dish, top with remaining sauce and sprinkle with cheeses.

2. Cover with aluminum foil and bake 25 minutes. Remove foil and bake an additional 5 minutes.   *Makes 4 to 6 servings*

Smart Tip

Brie cheese is called "soft-ripened" due to its soft texture. Select cheese that gives to gentle pressure and has an evenly colored, barely moist rind.

Baked Apricot Brie

Cook time: *14 minutes*

> 1 round (8 ounces) Brie cheese
> ⅓ cup apricot preserves
> 2 tablespoons sliced almonds
> Cracked pepper or other assorted crackers

1. Preheat oven to 400°F. Place cheese in small baking pan; spread top of cheese with preserves and sprinkle with almonds.

2. Bake about 10 to 12 minutes or until cheese begins to melt and lose its shape. Serve hot with crackers. Refrigerate leftovers; reheat before serving.

Makes 6 servings

Cherry Tomato Appetizers

> 1 pint cherry tomatoes
> Ice water
> ½ cup sliced green onions
> ¼ cup LAWRY'S® Lemon Pepper Marinade with Lemon Juice

In large pan of rapidly boiling water, carefully immerse tomatoes 15 seconds. Remove with slotted spoon and immediately submerge in ice water. Peel off and discard skins and stems. In large resealable plastic food storage bag, place tomatoes. Add green onions and Lemon Pepper Marinade; seal bag. Marinate in refrigerator at least 30 minutes. Serve cold.   *Makes 4 servings*

Serving Suggestion: Serve as an appetizer with wooden picks or as a side dish.

Right:
Baked Apricot Brie

Chunky Hawaiian Spread

        1 package (3 ounces) light cream cheese, softened
    ½ cup fat free or light sour cream
        1 can (8 ounces) DOLE® Crushed Pineapple, well-drained
    ¼ cup mango chutney*
        Low fat crackers

*If there are large pieces of fruit in chutney, cut into small pieces.

• Beat cream cheese, sour cream, pineapple and chutney in bowl until blended. Cover and chill 1 hour or overnight. Serve with crackers. Refrigerate any leftover spread in airtight container for up to one week.   *Makes 2½ cups*

Curried Buffalo Wings

    15 chicken wings (about 3 pounds)
    ¼ cup I CAN'T BELIEVE IT'S NOT BUTTER!® Spread
        1 tablespoon mild or hot curry powder
        2 teaspoons chopped garlic
        1 teaspoon salt

Preheat oven to 450°F.

Cut tips off chicken wings (save tips for soup). Cut chicken wings in half at joint; set aside.

In 12-inch skillet, melt I Can't Believe It's Not Butter! Spread over medium heat and cook curry, garlic and salt, stirring frequently, 30 seconds or until curry darkens slightly; set aside.

In bottom of broiler pan, without rack, pour curry sauce over chicken wings and toss to coat. Bake 35 minutes or until chicken wings are golden brown and fully cooked.   *Makes 30 appetizers*

Right:
Chunky Hawaiian Spread

Hot Buttered Cider
Prep and Cook Time: 15 *minutes*

¹⁄₃ **cup packed brown sugar**
¹⁄₄ **cup butter or margarine, softened**
¹⁄₄ **cup honey**
¹⁄₄ **teaspoon ground cinnamon**
¹⁄₄ **teaspoon ground nutmeg**
    Apple cider or juice

1. Beat sugar, butter, honey, cinnamon and nutmeg until well blended and fluffy. Place butter mixture in tightly covered container. Refrigerate up to 2 weeks. Bring butter mixture to room temperature before using.

2. To serve, heat apple cider in large saucepan over medium heat until hot. Fill individual mugs with hot apple cider; stir in 1 tablespoon butter mixture per 1 cup apple cider.   *Makes* 12 *servings*

Right:
Hot Buttered Cider

Above:
Spiced Apple Tea

Spiced Apple Tea

2 **cups unsweetened apple juice**
6 **whole cloves**
1 **cinnamon stick**
3 **cups water**
3 **bags cinnamon herbal tea**

Combine juice, cloves and cinnamon stick in medium saucepan. Bring to a boil over high heat. Reduce heat to low; simmer 10 minutes. Meanwhile, place water in another medium saucepan. Bring to a boil over high heat. Remove from heat; drop in tea bags and allow to steep for 6 minutes. Remove and discard tea bags.

Strain juice mixture; discard spices. Stir juice mixture into tea. Serve warm with additional cinnamon sticks, if desired, or refrigerate and serve cold over ice. (Tea may be made ahead, refrigerated, then reheated.)   *Makes* 4 *servings*

Quick Tip

To save time when thawing frozen strawberries, place them in the refrigerator the day before using them.

Right:
Strawberry Champagne Punch

Above:
V8® Bloody Mary Mocktail

Strawberry Champagne Punch

Prep Time: *15 minutes*

2 packages (10 ounces each) frozen sliced strawberries in syrup, thawed
2 cans (5½ ounces each) apricot or peach nectar
¼ cup lemon juice
2 tablespoons honey
2 bottles (750 ml each) champagne or sparkling white wine, chilled

1. Place strawberries with syrup in food processor; process until smooth.

2. Pour puréed strawberries into large punch bowl. Stir in apricot nectar, lemon juice and honey; blend well. Refrigerate until serving time.

3. To serve, stir champagne into strawberry mixture.　　*Makes 12 servings*

V8® Bloody Mary Mocktail

Prep Time: *5 minutes*

3 cups V8® 100% Vegetable Juice
1 teaspoon prepared horseradish
1 teaspoon Worcestershire sauce
½ teaspoon hot pepper sauce
Lemon slices for garnish

Mix vegetable juice, horseradish, Worcestershire sauce and hot pepper sauce. Serve over ice. Garnish with lemon slices.　　*Makes 3 cups*

Hot 'n' Spicy Mocktail: Increase prepared horseradish to 1 tablespoon.

Snowbird Mocktails
Prep Time: *10 minutes*

   3 cups pineapple juice
   1 can (14 ounces) sweetened condensed milk
   1 can (6 ounces) frozen orange juice concentrate, thawed
   ½ teaspoon coconut extract
   1 bottle (32 ounces) ginger ale, chilled

1. Combine pineapple juice, sweetened condensed milk, orange juice concentrate and coconut extract in large pitcher; stir well. Refrigerate, covered, up to 1 week.

2. To serve, pour ½ cup pineapple juice mixture into individual glasses (over crushed ice, if desired). Top off each glass with about ⅓ cup ginger ale.

Makes 10 servings

Cool Yogurt Smoothie
Prep Time: *5 minutes*

   1 container (8 ounces) BREYERS®* Lowfat Yogurt, any flavor
   2½ cups thawed COOL WHIP FREE® Whipped Topping, divided
   2 cups fresh or frozen strawberries or any other seasonal fruit, chopped
   2 cups ice cubes

BREYERS® is a registered trademark of Unilever, N.V., used under license.

PLACE yogurt, 1½ cups of the whipped topping, fruit and ice in blender container; cover. Blend until smooth. Top each serving with ¼ cup of the remaining whipped topping. Serve immediately.   *Makes 4 (1-cup) servings*

Smart Tip

Store unopened cans of sweetened condensed milk at room temperature up to 6 months. Once opened, store in airtight container in refrigerator for up to 5 days.

Right:
Snowbird Mocktails

Meat

Whether it's beef, pork or lamb, meat is perfect to serve for an entrée that's both substantial and delicious. These recipes use a variety of cooking methods and a delightful mix of ingredients. Try a different recipe every night. No one has to know that these great dishes are a snap to make!

Right:
Peppered Beef Rib Roast (recipe on page 42)

Quick Tip

Cut cleanup time and mess by lightly coating your broiler pan with vegetable oil or spraying it with nonstick cooking spray before you begin cooking.

Right:
Oriental Beef Kabobs

Oriental Beef Kabobs

1 tablespoon olive oil
1 tablespoon soy sauce
1 tablespoon seasoned rice vinegar
4 purchased beef kabobs

1. Preheat broiler. Position oven rack about 4 inches from heat source.

2. Whisk together oil, soy sauce and vinegar; brush mixture on kabobs.

3. Arrange kabobs on rack of broiler pan. Broil 10 minutes or to desired doneness, turning after 5 minutes.

Makes 4 servings

Orange-Pepper Steaks

2 teaspoons coarsely ground black pepper
4 beef tenderloin steaks, cut 1 inch thick
½ cup orange marmalade
4 teaspoons cider vinegar
½ teaspoon ground ginger
4 cups hot cooked rice

Press pepper evenly onto both sides of beef steaks. Place steaks on rack in broiler pan. Combine marmalade, vinegar and ginger in small bowl. Brush tops of steaks with half the marmalade mixture. Broil steaks 2 to 3 inches from heat, 10 to 15 minutes, turning once and brushing with remaining marmalade mixture. Serve over rice.

Makes 4 servings

Favorite recipe from **National Cattlemen's Beef Association**

Zesty Lemon-Glazed Steak

½ cup A.1.® Original or A.1.® BOLD & SPICY Steak Sauce
2 teaspoons grated lemon peel
1 clove garlic, minced
¼ teaspoon coarsely ground black pepper
¼ teaspoon dried oregano leaves
4 (4- to 6-ounce) beef shell steaks, about ½ inch thick

Blend steak sauce, lemon peel, garlic, pepper and oregano; brush on both sides of steaks. Grill steaks over medium heat or broil 6 inches from heat source 5 minutes on each side or to desired doneness, basting with sauce occasionally. Serve immediately.

Makes 4 servings

Barbecued Short Ribs

⅔ cup KIKKOMAN® Teriyaki Marinade & Sauce
¼ cup orange marmalade
1 teaspoon garlic salt
½ teaspoon lemon & pepper seasoning
5 pounds lean beef short ribs, 3 to 4 inches long

Combine teriyaki sauce, orange marmalade, garlic salt and lemon & pepper seasoning; pour over ribs in large bowl. Cover and refrigerate 8 to 10 hours or overnight, turning ribs over occasionally. Reserving marinade, remove ribs; place on grill 7 to 8 inches from hot coals. Cook 1½ to 2 hours, or until meat begins to pull away from bone, turning over frequently and brushing with reserved marinade during last 20 minutes of cooking time.

Makes 4 to 6 servings

Right:
*Zesty Lemon-
Glazed Steak*

Peppered Beef Rib Roast

1 ½ tablespoons black peppercorns
  1 boneless beef rib roast (2½ to 3 pounds), well trimmed
  ¼ cup Dijon mustard
  2 cloves garlic, minced
    Sour Cream Sauce (optional, recipe page 187)

Prepare grill for indirect cooking.

Place peppercorns in small resealable plastic food storage bag. Squeeze out excess air; close bag securely. Pound peppercorns until cracked using flat side of meat mallet or rolling pin. Set aside.

Pat roast dry with paper towels. Combine mustard and garlic in small bowl; brush onto top and sides of roast. Sprinkle pepper over mustard mixture.

Place roast, pepper side up, on grid directly over drip pan. Grill, covered, over medium heat 1 hour to 1 hour 10 minutes for medium or until internal temperature reaches 145°F when tested with meat thermometer inserted into thickest part of roast, adding 4 to 9 briquets to both sides of the fire after 45 minutes to maintain medium heat.

If desired, prepare Sour Cream Sauce. Cover; refrigerate until serving.

Transfer roast to cutting board; cover with foil. Let stand 10 to 15 minutes before carving. Internal temperature will continue to rise 5° to 10°F during stand time. Serve with Sour Cream Sauce.

Makes 6 to 8 servings

Smart Tip

For indirect grilling, the food is placed on the grid over a metal or disposable foil drip pan with coals banked either to one side or both sides of the pan. This method is used for slow-cooking foods, such as large roasts and whole chickens.

Oriental Flank Steak

½ cup WISH-BONE® Italian Dressing*
2 tablespoons soy sauce
2 tablespoons firmly packed brown sugar
½ teaspoon ground ginger (optional)
1 to 1½ pounds flank, top round or sirloin steak

*Also terrific with Wish-Bone® Robusto Italian or Just 2 Good Italian Dressing.

In nonaluminum dish, combine all ingredients except steak. Add steak; turn to coat. Cover and marinate in refrigerator 3 to 24 hours.

Remove steak, reserving marinade. Grill or broil until steak is done. Boil reserved marinade 1 minute; pour over steak.   *Makes 6 servings*

Above:
Oriental Flank Steak

Broccoli Beef

2 tablespoons vegetable oil
1 teaspoon chopped shallots
10 ounces sliced beef
6 tablespoons LEE KUM KEE® Stir-Fry Sauce, LEE KUM KEE® Spicy Stir-Fry Sauce or LEE KUM KEE® Stir-Fry Sauce Kung Pao, divided
1 cup cooked broccoli florets

Heat skillet over medium heat. Add oil. Stir-fry shallots. Add beef and 2 tablespoons Stir-Fry Sauce; stir-fry. When beef is half done, add broccoli and remaining 4 tablespoons Stir-Fry Sauce. Stir-fry until broccoli is crisp-tender,   *Makes 4 servings*

Cheese-Stuffed Meat Loaf

Prep Time: 20 *minutes*   **Cook Time:** 1 *hour*

1 ½ **pounds ground beef**
  1 **jar (26 to 28 ounces) RAGÚ® Chunky Gardenstyle Pasta Sauce**
  1 **large egg, slightly beaten**
¼ **cup plain dry bread crumbs**
  2 **cups shredded mozzarella cheese (about 8 ounces)**
  1 **tablespoon finely chopped fresh parsley**

1. Preheat oven to 350°F. In large bowl, combine ground beef, ⅓ cup Ragú Pasta Sauce, egg and bread crumbs. Season, if desired, with salt and ground black pepper. In 13×9-inch baking or roasting pan, shape into 12×8-inch rectangle.

2. Sprinkle 1½ cups cheese and parsley down center leaving ¾-inch border. Roll, starting at long end, jelly-roll style. Press ends together to seal.

3. Bake uncovered 45 minutes. Pour remaining sauce over meat loaf and sprinkle with remaining ½ cup cheese. Bake an additional 15 minutes or until sauce is heated through and cheese is melted. Let stand 5 minutes before serving.

Makes 6 servings

Tip: Molding the meat mixture onto waxed paper helps make rolling easier. Just lift waxed paper to curl the meat over cheese filling, then carefully remove meat from paper. Continue rolling in this manner until filling is enclosed in roll and meat is off paper.

Right:
*Cheese-Stuffed
Meat Loaf*

Ultimate Original Ranch® Cheese Burgers

**1 packet (1 ounce) HIDDEN VALLEY® Original Ranch® Salad
   Dressing & Recipe Mix**
1 pound ground beef
1 cup (4 ounces) shredded Cheddar cheese
4 large hamburger buns, toasted

Combine dressing mix with beef and cheese. Shape into 4 patties; cook thoroughly until no longer pink in center. Serve on toasted buns.   *Makes 4 servings*

Chuck Steak Teriyaki

1 (2½-pound) chuck steak, about 1½ inches thick
   Instant meat tenderizer
⅔ cup KIKKOMAN® Teriyaki Marinade & Sauce
1 can (6 ounces) tomato paste
¼ cup vegetable oil

Prepare steak with tenderizer according to package directions. Combine teriyaki sauce, tomato paste and vegetable oil. Place steak on grill 3 to 4 inches from hot coals; brush with teriyaki sauce mixture. Cook 15 minutes; turn over. Brush with teriyaki sauce mixture. Cook 10 minutes longer (for rare), or to desired doneness. (Or, place steak on rack of broiler pan; brush with teriyaki sauce mixture. Broil 10 minutes; turn over. Brush with teriyaki sauce mixture. Broil 10 minutes longer [for rare], or to desired doneness.) Heat remaining teriyaki sauce mixture; serve with steak.   *Makes 4 servings*

Smart Tip

For direct grilling, arrange hot coals in a single layer to extend 1 to 2 inches beyond the area of the food on the grid. This method is for quick-cooking foods, such as hamburgers, steaks, chicken breasts and fish.

Right:
Ultimate Original Ranch® Cheese Burgers

Cheesy Tacos

Prep Time: *5 minutes*   **Cook Time:** *15 minutes*

1 pound ground beef
¼ cup water
1 package (1 ¼ ounces) TACO BELL® HOME ORIGINALS™* Taco Seasoning Mix
¾ pound (12 ounces) VELVEETA® Mexican Pasteurized Process Cheese Spread with Jalapeño Peppers, cut up
1 package (4.5 ounces) TACO BELL® HOME ORIGINALS™* Taco Shells or 12 flour tortillas (8 inch)

*TACO BELL *and* HOME ORIGINALS *are registered trademarks owned and licensed by Taco Bell Corp.*

1. Brown meat in large skillet; drain. Stir in water and taco seasoning mix.

2. Add Velveeta; stir on low heat until Velveeta is melted.

3. Fill heated taco shells with meat mixture. Top with your favorite toppings, such as shredded lettuce, chopped tomato and Taco Bell Home Originals Thick 'N Chunky Salsa.   *Makes 4 to 6 servings*

Serving Suggestion: Cheesy Tacos are a fun family dinner. Have your child place the family's favorite taco toppings, such as shredded lettuce and chopped tomato, in a muffin tin to pass around at the table.

Below:
Cheesy Tacos

Citrus Grilled Steak

1 (6-ounce) can orange juice concentrate, thawed
½ cup A.1.® Steak Sauce
¼ cup dry sherry
1 clove garlic, minced
2 (8-ounce) beef club or strip steaks, about 1 inch thick

Blend orange juice concentrate, steak sauce, sherry and garlic. Place steaks in glass dish; coat with ½ cup orange juice mixture. Cover; refrigerate 1 hour, turning occasionally.

Heat remaining orange juice mixture in small saucepan over medium heat; keep warm.

Remove steaks from marinade; discard marinade. Grill over medium heat for 4 minutes on each side or until done, turning once. Serve steaks with reserved warm orange sauce.

Makes 4 servings

Above:
*Citrus Grilled
Steak*

Teriyaki Burgers

Prep Time: *5 minutes*   **Cook Time:** *15 minutes*

1 pound ground beef
3 tablespoons French's® Teriyaki Grill & Glaze Sauce

1. Combine beef with **Grill & Glaze** Sauce. Shape into 4 burgers.

2. Broil or grill burgers 10 minutes or until no longer pink in center, basting with additional **Grill & Glaze** Sauce.

Makes 4 servings

Campbell's® Best Ever Meatloaf

Prep Time: 10 *minutes*   **Cook Time:** 1 *hour* 20 *minutes*

1 can (10¾ ounces) CAMPBELL'S® Condensed Tomato Soup
2 pounds ground beef
1 pouch CAMPBELL'S® Dry Onion Soup and Recipe Mix
½ cup dry bread crumbs
1 egg, beaten
¼ cup water

1. Mix **½ cup** tomato soup, beef, onion soup mix, bread crumbs and egg **thoroughly.** In baking pan shape **firmly** into 8- by 4-inch loaf.

2. Bake at 350°F. for 1¼ hours or until meatloaf is no longer pink (160°F.).

3. In small saucepan mix **2 tablespoons** drippings, remaining tomato soup and water. Heat through. Serve with meatloaf.   *Makes 8 servings*

Grilled Steak au Poivre

½ cup A.1.® Steak Sauce, divided
1 (1½-pound) beef sirloin steak, ¾ inch thick
2 teaspoons cracked black pepper
½ cup dairy sour cream
2 tablespoons ketchup

Using 2 tablespoons steak sauce, brush both sides of steak; sprinkle 1 teaspoon pepper on each side, pressing into steak. Set aside.

Blend remaining steak sauce, sour cream and ketchup in medium saucepan. Cook and stir over low heat until heated through (do not boil); keep warm.

Grill steak over medium heat 5 minutes on each side or until done. Serve steak with warm sauce.   *Makes 6 servings*

Smart Tip

Choose fresh meat that has good color (pink for pork, veal and lamb; red for beef). Avoid meat that is pale or gray-colored. Any fat should be firm and creamy white, not yellow. The meat should have no odd odors.

Right:
Campbell's® Best Ever Meatloaf

Skewered Beef Strips with Spicy Honey Glaze

Prep and Cook Time: *30 minutes*

  1 **pound beef top sirloin steak**
  ⅓ **cup soy sauce**
  2 **tablespoons white vinegar**
  1 **teaspoon ground ginger**
  ⅛ **teaspoon ground red pepper**
  ⅓ **cup honey**

1. Slice beef across grain into ¼-inch-thick strips. Thread beef strips onto 12 wooden skewers and place in large glass baking dish. (Soak skewers in cold water 20 minutes before using to prevent them from burning.)

2. Heat broiler or prepare grill. Combine soy sauce, vinegar, ginger and ground red pepper; pour over skewers and marinate 10 minutes, turning once.

3. Drain marinade into small saucepan; stir in honey and brush mixture over beef. Bring remaining mixture to a boil; boil 2 minutes.

4. Broil or grill skewered beef 3 to 4 minutes. Serve remaining honey glaze as dipping sauce.   *Makes 4 servings*

Prime Ribs of Beef à la Lawry's®

  1 **(8-pound) prime rib roast**
    LAWRY'S® Seasoned Salt
    Rock salt

Preheat oven to 500°F.

Score fat on meat and rub generously with Seasoned Salt. Cover bottom of roasting pan with rock salt 1 inch deep. Place roast directly on rock salt and bake, uncovered, 8 minutes per pound for rare.   *Makes 8 servings*

Right:
Skewered Beef Strips with Spicy Honey Glaze

Rolled Steak Stuffed with Asparagus

1 pound fresh California asparagus
2 tablespoons prepared horseradish
2 tablespoons minced garlic
2 to 4 pounds flank steak, butterflied, opened

Spread horseradish and garlic on steak. Arrange asparagus spears in single row over spread. Roll tightly and tie. Place steak in roasting pan.

Roast in 350°F oven 1 hour. Remove from oven and let stand 10 minutes before slicing.

Makes 8 to 10 servings

Favorite recipe from **California Asparagus Commission**

Right:
*Rolled Steak
Stuffed with
Asparagus*

Above:
*Jalapeño Pepper
Steak*

Jalapeño Pepper Steak

Prep Time: 15 *minutes*   **Cook Time:** 10 *minutes*

1 pound sirloin steak or boneless chicken, cut into strips
1 package (16 ounces) frozen bell pepper and onion strips, thawed and drained *or* 3 cups fresh bell pepper and onion strips
¾ pound (12 ounces) VELVEETA® Mexican Pasteurized Process Cheese Spread with Jalapeño Peppers, cut up

1. Spray large skillet with no stick cooking spray. Add steak; cook on high heat 2 minutes or until no longer pink; remove from skillet.

2. Stir in vegetables; cook 2 minutes. Reduce heat to medium-low.

3. Add Velveeta; stir until melted. Stir in steak. Serve over hot cooked MINUTE® White Rice or on tortillas.

Makes 6 servings

Easy Pleasing Meatloaf
Prep Time: 10 minutes   **Bake Time:** 1 hour

  2 pounds lean ground beef or turkey
  1 package (6¼ ounces) STOVE TOP® Stuffing Mix for Beef
  2 eggs, beaten
  ½ cup catsup, divided

MIX 1 cup of water and all ingredients except ¼ cup of the catsup.

SHAPE meat mixture into oval loaf in center of 13×9-inch baking dish; top with remaining ¼ cup catsup.

BAKE at 375°F for 1 hour or until center is no longer pink.   *Makes 6 to 8 servings*

Note: Recipe can be doubled. Prepare as directed, shaping meat mixture into 2 loaves. Place loaves, side by side, in 13×9-inch baking dish. Bake at 375°F for 1 hour and 25 minutes. Use leftover meatloaf to make sandwiches.

Onion-Baked Pork Chops

  1 envelope LIPTON® RECIPE SECRETS® Golden Onion Soup Mix*
  ⅓ cup plain dry bread crumbs
  4 pork chops, 1 inch thick (about 3 pounds)
  1 egg, well beaten

Also terrific with LIPTON® RECIPE SECRETS® Onion, Savory Herb with Garlic or Fiesta Herb with Red Pepper Soup Mix.

1. Preheat oven to 400°F. In small bowl, combine soup mix and bread crumbs. Dip chops in egg, then bread crumb mixture, until evenly coated.

2. In lightly greased 13×9-inch baking or roasting pan, arrange chops.

3. Bake, uncovered, 20 minutes or until done, turning once.   *Makes 4 servings*

Serving Tip

To serve a more attractive, ample meatloaf, remember: the higher the fat content in the raw ground beef or turkey used, the more shrinkage will occur after cooking. Buy leaner product to get a fuller loaf.

Right:
Onion-Baked Pork Chop

Lemon-Capered Pork Tenderloin

1 ½ **pounds boneless pork tenderloin**
  1 **tablespoon crushed capers**
  1 **teaspoon dried rosemary**
⅛ **teaspoon black pepper**
  1 **cup water**
¼ **cup lemon juice**

1. Preheat oven to 350°F. Trim fat from tenderloin; discard. Set tenderloin aside.

2. Combine capers, rosemary and black pepper in small bowl. Rub rosemary mixture over tenderloin. Place tenderloin in shallow roasting pan. Pour combined water and lemon juice over tenderloin.

3. Bake, uncovered, 1 hour or until thermometer inserted in thickest part of tenderloin registers 170°F. Remove from oven; cover with aluminum foil. Allow to stand 10 minutes before serving. Garnish as desired.   *Makes 8 servings*

Fantastic Pork Fajitas

  2 **teaspoons vegetable oil**
  1 **pound pork strips**
½ **medium onion, peeled and sliced**
  1 **green bell pepper, seeded and sliced**
  4 **flour tortillas, warmed**

Heat large nonstick skillet over medium-high heat. Add oil; heat until hot. Add pork strips, onion and bell pepper slices and stir-fry quickly 4 to 5 minutes or until pork is barely pink and vegetables are crisp-tender. Roll up portions of the meat mixture in flour tortillas and serve with purchased salsa, if desired.

Makes 4 servings

Favorite recipe from **National Pork Producers Council**

Right:
Lemon-Capered
Pork Tenderloin

Peachy Pork Roast

1 (3- to 4-pound) rolled boneless pork loin roast
1 cup (12-ounce jar) SMUCKER'S® Currant Jelly
½ cup SMUCKER'S® Peach Preserves
   Fresh or canned peach slices and currants for garnish, if desired

Place pork in roasting pan; insert meat thermometer into one end of roast. Bake at 325°F for 30 to 40 minutes or until browned. Turn roast over; bake additional 30 minutes to brown the bottom. Turn roast again and drain off drippings.

In saucepan over medium heat, melt currant jelly and peach preserves; set aside about ½ cup of mixture.

Brush roast generously with remaining sauce. Bake until thermometer reads 160°F, about 15 minutes, basting occasionally with sauce.

Remove from oven. Garnish with peach slices and currants, if desired. Serve with sauce.

Makes 8 to 10 servings

Right:
Peachy Pork Roast

Pork Medallions with Marsala

1 pound pork tenderloin, cut into ½-inch slices
  All-purpose flour
2 tablespoons olive oil
1 clove garlic, minced
½ cup sweet Marsala wine
2 tablespoons chopped fresh parsley

Lightly dust pork with flour. Heat oil in large skillet over medium-high heat until hot. Add pork slices; cook 3 minutes per side or until browned. Remove from pan. Reduce heat to medium. Add garlic to skillet; cook and stir 1 minute. Add wine and pork; cook 3 minutes or until pork is barely pink in center. Remove pork from skillet. Stir in parsley. Simmer wine mixture until slightly thickened, 2 to 3 minutes.

Makes 4 servings

Above:
Pork Medallions with Marsala

Right:
*Maple-Cranberry
Pork Chop*

Smart Tip

*Adding wine
or any other
liquid to a
pan that was
just used to
cook meat—a
process called
"deglazing"
— removes
cooked-on
food from the
pan and adds
a rich flavor
to sauces.*

Maple-Cranberry Pork Chops

Prep and Cook Time: *20 minutes*

4 well-trimmed center cut pork chops ($\frac{1}{2}$ inch thick)
1 cup dry red wine or apple juice
$\frac{1}{2}$ cup pure maple syrup or maple-flavored syrup
$\frac{1}{2}$ cup dried cranberries
1 tablespoon cold water
2 teaspoons cornstarch

1. Spray large nonstick skillet with nonstick cooking spray. Heat skillet over medium-high heat until hot. Add pork chops; cook 3 to 5 minutes per side or just until browned and pork is no longer pink in center. Remove from skillet; keep warm.

2. Add wine, syrup and cranberries to skillet; cook and stir over medium-high heat 2 to 3 minutes.

3. Combine water and cornstarch in small bowl; stir until smooth. Add cornstarch mixture to skillet; cook and stir about 1 minute or until thickened and clear. Reduce heat to medium. Return pork chops to skillet; spoon sauce over and simmer 1 minute.

Makes 4 servings

Sweet and Sour Pork

Prep Time: *5 minutes*   **Cook Time:** *15 to 18 minutes*

¾ **pound boneless pork**
1 **teaspoon vegetable oil**
1 **bag (16 ounces) BIRDS EYE® frozen Farm Fresh Mixtures Pepper Stir Fry vegetables**
1 **tablespoon water**
1 **jar (14 ounces) sweet and sour sauce**
1 **can (8 ounces) pineapple chunks, drained**

• Cut pork into thin strips.

• In large skillet, heat oil over medium-high heat.

• Add pork; stir-fry until pork is browned.

• Add vegetables and water; cover and cook over medium heat 5 to 7 minutes or until vegetables are crisp-tender.

• Uncover; stir in sweet and sour sauce and pineapple. Cook until heated through.

Makes 4 servings

Serving Suggestion: Serve over hot cooked rice.

Quick Tip

For a quick sweet and sour sauce for chicken nuggets or egg rolls, add sugar and vinegar to taste to jarred strained apricots or peaches.

Right:
Sweet and Sour Pork

Cider Glazed Pork Roast

  1 **pork loin roast (4 to 5 pounds), boned and tied**
½ **cup apple cider**
¼ **cup Dijon-style mustard**
¼ **cup vegetable oil**
¼ **cup soy sauce**

Insert meat thermometer in center of thickest part of roast. Arrange medium-hot KINGSFORD® Briquets around drip pan. Place roast over drip pan. Cover grill and cook 2½ to 3 hours, or until thermometer registers 170°F, adding more briquets as necessary. Combine apple cider, mustard, oil and soy sauce. Brush roast with cider mixture 3 or 4 times during last 30 minutes of cooking.   *Makes 6 servings*

Lite Teriyaki Pork Chops

½ **cup KIKKOMAN® Lite Teriyaki Marinade & Sauce**
  2 **tablespoons prepared horseradish**
⅛ **teaspoon ground cinnamon**
  4 **pork rib or loin chops, ¾ inch thick**

Blend lite teriyaki sauce, horseradish and cinnamon; pour over chops in large plastic food storage bag. Press air out of bag; close top securely. Turn bag over several times to coat all chops well. Refrigerate 1½ hours, turning bag over occasionally. Reserving marinade, remove chops. Place chops on grill 5 to 7 inches from medium-hot coals. Cook 10 to 12 minutes, or until light pink in center, turning over and brushing occasionally with reserved marinade. (Or, place chops on rack of broiler pan. Broil 5 to 7 inches from heat 8 to 10 minutes, or until light pink in center, turning over and brushing occasionally with reserved marinade.)   *Makes 4 servings*

Serving Tip

Allow a roast to rest for 10 to 15 minutes (covered lightly with foil) after cooking to allow juices in the center of the roast to redistribute throughout the meat. Carving will be easier and all the meat will be uniformly tender.

Peachy Pork Picante

4 boneless top loin pork chops, cubed
2 tablespoons taco seasoning
1 cup salsa
4 tablespoons peach preserves

Toss pork with taco seasoning; lightly brown pork in a non-stick skillet over medium-high heat; stir in salsa and preserves. Bring to a boil; lower heat. Cover and simmer 8 to 10 minutes.

Makes 4 servings

Favorite recipe from **National Pork Producers Council**

Above:
*Peachy Pork
Picante*

Lemon Pepper Lamb Kabobs

1 ½ cups LAWRY'S® Lemon Pepper Marinade with Lemon Juice, divided
1 ½ pounds boneless lamb loin roast, cut into 1 ½-inch cubes
12 mushrooms
2 green bell peppers, cut into chunks
2 onions, cut into wedges

In large resealable plastic food storage bag, combine 1 cup Lemon Pepper Marinade and lamb; seal bag. Marinate in refrigerator at least 30 minutes. Remove lamb; discard used marinade. Alternately thread lamb and vegetables onto skewers. Grill or broil skewers 8 to 10 minutes or until desired doneness, turning once and basting often with additional ½ cup Lemon Pepper Marinade. *Do not baste during last 5 minutes of cooking.* Discard any remaining marinade.

Makes 6 servings

Serving Suggestion: Serve over a bed of couscous with a Greek salad.

Rack of Lamb with Dijon-Mustard Sauce

1 rack of lamb (3 pounds), all visible fat removed
1 cup finely chopped fresh parsley
½ cup Dijon mustard
½ cup soft whole wheat bread crumbs
1 tablespoon chopped fresh rosemary *or* 2 teaspoons dried rosemary
1 teaspoon minced garlic
Fresh rosemary, lemon slices and lemon peel strips (optional)

Preheat oven to 500°F. Place lamb in large baking pan. Combine parsley, mustard, bread crumbs, rosemary and garlic in small bowl. Spread evenly over top of lamb. Place in center of oven; cook 7 minutes for medium-rare. Turn off oven but do not open door for at least 30 minutes. Serve 2 to 3 chops on each plate, depending on size and total number of chops. Garnish with additional fresh rosemary, lemon slices and lemon peel strips, if desired. *Makes 6 servings*

Lemon Pepper & Thyme Rub

¼ cup minced fresh thyme leaves
1 tablespoon LAWRY'S® Lemon Pepper
2 teaspoons LAWRY'S® Seasoned Salt
1 pound lamb chops
2 tablespoons olive oil

In small bowl, combine thyme, Lemon Pepper and Seasoned Salt; mix well. Brush both sides of chops with oil. Sprinkle with thyme mixture, pressing onto chops. Grill or broil chops 10 to 12 minutes or until desired doneness, turning halfway through grilling time. *Makes 4 servings*

Serving Suggestion: Serve with garlic mashed potatoes and steamed asparagus.

Hint: Also excellent on beef, pork or chicken.

Right:
Rack of Lamb with Dijon-Mustard Sauce

Roast Leg of Lamb

3 tablespoons coarse-grained mustard
2 cloves garlic, minced*
1 ½ teaspoons dried rosemary leaves, crushed
½ teaspoon black pepper
1 leg of lamb, well trimmed, boned, rolled and tied (about 4 pounds)
Mint jelly (optional)

For more intense garlic flavor inside the meat, cut garlic into slivers. Cut small pockets at random intervals throughout roast with tip of sharp knife; insert garlic slivers.

Preheat oven to 400°F. Combine mustard, garlic, rosemary and pepper. Rub mustard mixture over lamb.** Place roast on meat rack in shallow, foil-lined roasting pan. Roast 15 minutes. *Reduce oven temperature to 325°F;* roast about 20 minutes per pound for medium or until internal temperature reaches 145°F when tested with meat thermometer inserted into thickest part of roast, not touching bone.

Transfer roast to cutting board; cover with foil. Let stand 10 to 15 minutes before carving. Internal temperature will continue to rise 5° to 10°F during stand time.

Cut strings; discard. Carve roast into thin slices; serve with mint jelly, if desired.

Makes 10 to 12 servings

**At this point lamb may be covered and refrigerated up to 24 hours before roasting.*

Smart Tip

Choose firm, dry heads of garlic with tightly closed cloves and smooth skin. Avoid garlic with sprouting green shoots. Store, unwrapped, in a cool, dry, dark place with good ventilation for up to 3 months.

Right:
Roast Leg of Lamb

Poultry

Chicken and turkey dishes are a regular part of most family diets and with good reason: they offer unlimited possibilities for creating sensational quick meals. Whether you're making great grilled dishes, captivating casseroles or stimulating stews, poultry is sure to please.

Right:
*Chicken Parmesan
(recipe on page 90)*

Mile-High Enchilada Pie

8 (6-inch) corn tortillas
1 jar (12 ounces) prepared salsa
1 can (15½ ounces) kidney beans, rinsed and drained
1 cup shredded cooked chicken
1 cup shredded Monterey Jack cheese with jalapeño peppers

Slow Cooker Directions: Prepare foil handles for slow cooker (see note below); place in slow cooker. Place 1 tortilla on bottom of slow cooker. Top with small amount of salsa, beans, chicken and cheese. Continue layering, using remaining ingredients, ending with cheese. Cover and cook on Low 6 to 8 hours or on High 3 to 4 hours. Pull out by foil handles. *Makes 4 to 6 servings*

Foil Handles: Tear off three 18×2-inch strips of heavy foil or use regular foil folded to double thickness. Crisscross foil strips in spoke design and place in slow cooker to make lifting of tortilla stack easier.

Crispy Onion Chicken Fingers
Prep and Cook Time: *25 minutes*

1⅓ cups *French's® Taste Toppers™* French Fried Onions
1 pound boneless skinless chicken fingers
3 to 4 tablespoons *French's®* Honey Mustard

1. Preheat oven to 400°F. Crush **Taste Toppers** with rolling pin.

2. Coat chicken fingers with mustard. Dip into crushed **Taste Toppers**. Place chicken on baking sheet.

3. Bake 15 minutes or until chicken is crispy and no longer pink in center.

Makes 4 servings

Note: Boneless chicken breast halves may be substituted for the fingers. Bake until chicken is no longer pink in center.

Smart Tip

Regardless of the cooking methods used, always cook chicken completely. Do not partially cook it and then store it to finish cooking later.

Right:
Mile-High Enchilada Pie

Citrus Chicken

1 large orange
1 large lime
¾ cup WISH-BONE® Italian Dressing
2½ to 3 pounds chicken pieces

From the orange, grate enough peel to measure 1½ teaspoons and squeeze enough juice to measure ⅓ cup; set aside.

From the lime, grate enough peel to measure 1 teaspoon* and squeeze enough juice to measure 3 tablespoons; set aside.

For marinade, combine Italian dressing, orange and lime juices and orange and lime peels. In large, shallow nonaluminum baking dish or plastic bag, pour ¾ cup marinade over chicken; turn to coat. Cover, or close bag, and marinate in refrigerator, turning occasionally, 3 to 24 hours. Refrigerate remaining ½ cup marinade.

Remove chicken from marinade, discarding marinade. Grill or broil chicken, turning once and brushing frequently with refrigerated marinade, until chicken is no longer pink in center.   *Makes 4 servings*

*Lime peel may be omitted. Use only 3 tablespoons lime juice.

Variation: Also terrific with WISH-BONE® Robusto Italian or Just 2 Good Italian Dressing.

Fresco Marinated Chicken

1 envelope LIPTON® RECIPE SECRETS® Garlic Mushroom Soup Mix*
1/3 cup water
1/4 cup olive or vegetable oil
1 teaspoon lemon juice or vinegar
4 boneless, skinless chicken breast halves (about 1 1/4 pounds)

*Also terrific with LIPTON® RECIPE SECRETS® Savory Herb with Garlic or Golden Onion Soup Mix.

1. For marinade, blend all ingredients except chicken.

2. In shallow baking dish or plastic bag, pour 1/2 cup of marinade over chicken. Cover, or close bag, and marinate in refrigerator, turning occasionally, up to 3 hours. Refrigerate remaining marinade.

3. Remove chicken, discarding marinade. Grill or broil chicken, turning once and brushing with refrigerated marinade, until chicken is no longer pink in center.

Makes 4 servings

Above:
Fresco Marinated Chicken

Cutlets Milanese

Prep Time: *6 to 8 minutes*   **Cook Time:** *6 minutes*

1 package (about 1 pound) PERDUE® FIT 'N EASY® Fresh Thin-Sliced
    Chicken or Turkey Breast Cutlets
Salt and ground pepper to taste
1/2 cup Italian seasoned bread crumbs
1/2 cup grated Parmesan cheese
1 large egg beaten with 1 teaspoon water
2 to 3 tablespoons olive oil

Season cutlets with salt and pepper. On wax paper, combine bread crumbs and Parmesan cheese. Dip cutlets in egg mixture and dredge in bread crumb mixture. In large, nonstick skillet over medium-high heat, heat oil. Add cutlets and sauté 3 minutes per side, until golden brown and cooked through. *Makes 4 servings*

Cheesy Chicken Pot Pie

1 pound boneless, skinless chicken breast halves, cut into ½-inch chunks
1 tablespoon all-purpose flour
1 jar (16 ounces) RAGÚ® Cheese Creations!® Double Cheddar Sauce
1 bag (16 ounces) frozen mixed vegetables, thawed
1 prepared pastry for single-crust pie

Preheat oven to 425°F. In 2-quart casserole, toss chicken with flour. Stir in Ragú Cheese Creations! Sauce and vegetables. Cover casserole with prepared pastry. Press pastry around edge of casserole to seal; trim excess pastry, then flute edges. Cover with aluminum foil and bake 20 minutes. Remove foil and continue baking 20 minutes or until crust is golden and chicken is no longer pink in center. Let stand 5 minutes before serving. *Makes 6 servings*

Tip: This is the perfect dish for leftovers. Substitute cooked pork roast, turkey breast or even roast beef for the chicken.

Hawaiian Chicken
Prep Time: 5 minutes **Cook Time:** 15 minutes

1 tablespoon oil
1 pound boneless chicken breasts, cut into 2-inch pieces
1 can (20 ounces) pineapple chunks in their own juice
½ cup French's® Honey Mustard Grill & Glaze Sauce
1 green or red bell pepper, cut into chunks

1. Heat 1 tablespoon oil in nonstick skillet over medium-high heat. Cook chicken until browned; drain.

2. Add remaining ingredients. Bring to a boil. Reduce heat to medium-low; simmer 5 to 8 minutes or until chicken is no longer pink in center and sauce thickens slightly. Serve with rice, if desired. *Makes 4 servings*

Smart Tip

To avoid contaminating other foods with salmonella bacteria, thoroughly wash cutting surfaces, utensils and your hands with hot soapy water after they touch uncooked chicken. Cooking kills salmonella.

Right:
Cheesy Chicken Pot Pie

Chicken and Asparagus Hollandaise

Prep Time: 10 *minutes*　　**Cook Time:** 20 *to* 25 *minutes*

1 package (1.25 ounces) hollandaise sauce mix
1 pound boneless chicken breasts, cut into strips
2 teaspoons lemon juice
1 box (10 ounces) BIRDS EYE® frozen Asparagus
　Dash cayenne pepper

• Prepare hollandaise sauce according to package directions.

• Spray large skillet with nonstick cooking spray; cook chicken strips over medium-high heat 10 to 12 minutes or until browned, stirring occasionally.

• Add hollandaise sauce, lemon juice and asparagus. Cover and cook, stirring occasionally, 5 to 10 minutes or until asparagus is heated through. (Do not overcook.)

• Add cayenne pepper, and salt and black pepper to taste.　　*Makes 4 to 6 servings*

Apricot-Glazed Chicken

$\frac{1}{2}$ cup WISH-BONE® Italian Dressing
2 teaspoons ground ginger (optional)
1 chicken, cut into serving pieces (2$\frac{1}{2}$ to 3 pounds)
$\frac{1}{4}$ cup apricot or peach preserves

In large, shallow nonaluminum baking dish or plastic bag, blend Italian dressing and ginger. Add chicken; turn to coat. Cover, or close bag, and marinate in refrigerator, turning occasionally, 3 hours or overnight. Remove chicken, reserving $\frac{1}{4}$ cup marinade.

In small saucepan, bring reserved marinade to a boil and continue boiling 1 minute. Remove from heat and stir in preserves until melted; set aside. Grill or broil chicken until chicken is no longer pink near bone, brushing with preserve mixture during last 5 minutes of cooking.　　*Makes 4 servings*

Right:
Chicken and Asparagus Hollandaise

Campbell's® Lemon Asparagus Chicken
Prep and Cook Time: 20 *minutes*

1 tablespoon vegetable oil
4 skinless, boneless chicken breast halves (about 1 pound)
1 can (10¾ ounces) CAMPBELL'S® Condensed Cream of Asparagus Soup
¼ cup milk
1 tablespoon lemon juice
⅛ teaspoon pepper

1. In medium skillet over medium-high heat, heat oil. Add chicken and cook 8 minutes or until browned. Set chicken aside. Pour off fat.

2. Add soup, milk, lemon juice and pepper. Heat to a boil. Return chicken to pan. Reduce heat to low. Cover and cook 5 minutes or until chicken is no longer pink.

Makes 4 servings

Chile Rellenos-Style Chicken
Prep Time: 5 *minutes*   **Cook Time:** 25 *minutes*

6 boneless skinless chicken breast halves
1 envelope SHAKE 'N BAKE® Seasoning and Coating Mixture— Hot & Spicy Recipe for Chicken
½ cup (2 ounces) shredded Cheddar or Monterey Jack cheese*
1 can (4 ounces) chopped green chilies, drained
Salsa (optional)

*Or, use ¼ cup of each cheese.

HEAT oven to 400°F.

COAT chicken with coating mixture as directed on package.

BAKE 20 minutes on ungreased or foil-lined 15×10-inch metal baking pan. Mix cheese and chilies. Spoon over chicken. Bake 5 minutes or until chicken is cooked through and cheese is melted. Serve with salsa. *Makes 4 servings*

Quick Tip

If you skin and debone chicken breasts, reserve both the bones and skin. Place them in a plastic bag and freeze them; soon you'll have enough to make flavorful homemade chicken stock.

Right, top to bottom: Campbell's® Asparagus & Ham Potato Topper (page 16) and Campbell's® Lemon Asparagus Chicken

Garlic 'n Lemon Roast Chicken

1 small onion, finely chopped
1 envelope LIPTON® RECIPE SECRETS® Savory Herb with Garlic
Soup Mix*
2 tablespoons olive or vegetable oil
2 tablespoons lemon juice
1 (3½-pound) roasting chicken

Also terrific with LIPTON® RECIPE SECRETS® Fiesta Herb with Red Pepper Soup Mix.

1. In large plastic bag or bowl, combine onion and soup mix blended with oil and lemon juice; add chicken. Close bag and shake, or toss in bowl, until chicken is evenly coated. Cover and marinate in refrigerator, turning occasionally, 2 hours.

2. Preheat oven to 350°F. Place chicken and marinade in 13×9-inch baking or roasting pan. Arrange chicken, breast side up; discard bag.

3. Bake uncovered, basting occasionally, 1 hour and 20 minutes or until meat thermometer reaches 180°F. (Insert meat thermometer into thickest part of thigh between breast and thigh; be sure tip does not touch bone.)   *Makes 4 servings*

Jalapeño Grilled Chicken

2 packages BUTTERBALL® Chicken Split Breasts
¼ cup jalapeño jelly
2 tablespoons fresh lime juice

Combine jalapeño jelly and lime juice in small saucepan. Heat over medium heat, stirring constantly, until melted and smooth. Grill chicken breasts 15 to 20 minutes on each side or until internal temperature reaches 170°F and chicken is no longer pink in center. Brush jalapeño mixture on chicken during last 10 minutes of grilling.   *Makes 6 servings*

Right:
*Garlic 'n Lemon
Roast Chicken*

Tangy Grilled Chicken Kabobs

Prep Time: 10 *minutes plus marinating*　　**Grill Time:** 15 *minutes*

1 cup MIRACLE WHIP LIGHT® Dressing
1 envelope GOOD SEASONS® Italian Salad Dressing Mix
2 tablespoons vinegar
2 tablespoons water
1 ½ pounds boneless skinless chicken breast halves, cut into 1 ½-inch pieces
　　Assorted cut-up fresh vegetables (peppers, mushrooms, onions and zucchini)

MIX dressing, salad dressing mix, vinegar and water in cruet or small bowl. Reserve ½ cup for dipping cooked kabobs.

ARRANGE chicken and vegetables on 6 skewers. Pour remaining dressing mixture over skewers in shallow dish. Refrigerate 30 minutes to marinate. Remove kabobs from marinade; discard marinade.

PLACE kabobs on grill over medium-hot coals. Grill 10 to 15 minutes or until chicken is no longer pink in center, turning once. Serve with reserved ½ cup dressing mixture.

Makes 6 servings

Variation: Omit grilling. Heat broiler. Place kabobs on rack of broiler pan; brush with dressing mixture. Broil 5 to 7 inches from heat 10 to 15 minutes or until chicken is no longer pink in center.

Smart Tip

Long, thin wooden skewers work well for grilling individual servings consisting of small pieces of poultry, meat, vegetables and fruits. Soak skewers in water for about 30 minutes before using to prevent burning.

Right:
Tangy Grilled Chicken Kabob

Crispy Oven-Baked Chicken

4 boneless skinless chicken breast halves (about 4 ounces each)
¾ cup GUILTLESS GOURMET® Roasted Red Pepper Salsa
   Nonstick cooking spray
1 cup (3.5 ounces) crushed* GUILTLESS GOURMET® Baked Tortilla
     Chips (yellow corn, red corn or chili lime)
   Cherry tomatoes and pineapple sage leaves (optional)

*Crush tortilla chips in the original bag or between two pieces of waxed paper with a rolling pin.

Wash chicken; pat dry with paper towels. Place chicken in shallow nonmetal pan or place in large resealable plastic food storage bag. Pour salsa over chicken. Cover with foil or seal bag; marinate in refrigerator 8 hours or overnight.

Preheat oven to 350°F. Coat baking sheet with cooking spray. Place crushed chips on waxed paper. Remove chicken from salsa, discarding salsa; roll chicken in crushed chips. Place on prepared baking sheet; bake 45 minutes or until chicken is no longer pink in center and chips are crisp. Serve hot. Garnish with tomatoes and sage, if desired. *Makes 4 servings*

Right:
Crispy Oven-Baked Chicken

Saucy Chicken

2 pounds chicken breasts
1 (8-ounce) bottle Russian or French salad dressing
1 (1.25-ounce) envelope onion soup mix (dry)
1 cup (12-ounce jar) SMUCKER'S® Apricot Preserves
   Hot cooked rice (optional)

Place chicken, skin side up, in 13×9-inch baking pan. Combine dressing, soup mix and preserves; mix well. Pour over chicken.

Bake at 350° for 1 hour or until chicken is fork-tender and juices run clear; halfway through cooking time, spoon sauce over breasts. Serve over hot cooked rice, if desired. *Makes 8 servings*

Chicken Parmesan

Prep and Cook Time: *30 minutes*

4 boneless, skinless chicken breast halves
2 cans (14½ ounces each) DEL MONTE® Italian Recipe Stewed Tomatoes
2 tablespoons cornstarch
½ teaspoon dried oregano or basil, crushed
¼ teaspoon hot pepper sauce (optional)
¼ cup grated Parmesan cheese

1. Preheat oven to 425°F. Slightly flatten each chicken breast; place in 11×7-inch baking dish.

2. Cover with foil; bake 20 minutes or until chicken is no longer pink in center. Remove foil; drain.

3. Meanwhile, in large saucepan, combine tomatoes, cornstarch, oregano and pepper sauce. Stir to dissolve cornstarch. Cook, stirring constantly, until thickened.

4. Pour sauce over chicken; top with cheese.

5. Return to oven; bake, uncovered, 5 minutes or until cheese is melted. Garnish with chopped parsley and serve with rice or pasta, if desired.   *Makes 4 servings*

Serving Tip

When planning a menu, select the entrée first and then pair it with dishes that will complement it in appearance. For instance, a very simple rice or pasta side dish would look attractive alongside an entrée that has red sauce.

Drums of Heaven

1 tablespoon KIKKOMAN® Soy Sauce
1 tablespoon dry sherry
18 chicken wing drumettes
⅓ cup KIKKOMAN® Teriyaki Baste & Glaze
1 large clove garlic, minced
2 teaspoons sesame seed, toasted

Preheat oven to 425°F. Combine soy sauce and sherry in large bowl; add drumettes. Toss until well coated. Arrange drumettes, in single layer, on large rack in shallow foil-lined baking pan. Bake 30 minutes. Meanwhile, combine teriyaki baste & glaze and garlic in small bowl; brush tops of drumettes with half of glaze. Turn pieces over; brush with remaining glaze. Bake 15 minutes longer or until browned and juices run clear; sprinkle with sesame seed.   *Makes 6 servings*

Original Ranch® Broiled Chicken

1 packet (1 ounce) HIDDEN VALLEY® Original Ranch® Salad Dressing &
   Recipe Mix
2 tablespoons olive oil
1 tablespoon red wine vinegar
1 pound boneless, skinless chicken breasts and/or thighs

Combine salad dressing & recipe mix, oil and vinegar in a resealable plastic bag. Add chicken; shake, working mixture into meat. Marinate 1 hour in refrigerator. Broil chicken about 10 to14 minutes total, turning once, or until no longer pink in center.   *Makes 4 servings*

French Pan-Roasted Hens

1 package (about 3 pounds) PERDUE® Fresh Split Cornish Hens
3 tablespoons olive oil, divided
1 tablespoon herbes de Provence
  Salt and black pepper
3 garlic cloves, peeled, divided
½ cup white wine or water

Rub hens with 1 tablespoon oil; sprinkle with herbes de Provence, and salt and pepper to taste. Heat remaining 2 tablespoons oil in large, deep skillet over medium-high heat. Add hens and 2 garlic cloves. Brown hens lightly on both sides. Discard cooked garlic and add remaining garlic clove. Reduce heat to low; cover and cook 30 to 40 minutes until hens are browned and juices run clear, turning 2 to 3 times.

Remove hens to warm serving platter; discard garlic. Add wine to skillet; cook 1 minute, stirring to incorporate pan juices. Serve hens with pan sauce.

Makes 2 to 4 servings

Mediterranean Carrots with Chicken
Prep Time: 5 *minutes*   **Cook Time:** 20 *minutes*

2 boxes (10 ounces each) BIRDS EYE® frozen Deluxe Baby Whole Carrots
2 cups cubed cooked chicken breasts
3 tablespoons brown sugar
2 tablespoons lemon juice
1 teaspoon cumin

• In large saucepan, combine all ingredients. Cover; cook over medium-low heat 20 minutes or until chicken is heated through and carrots are tender.

Makes 4 servings

Smart Tip

Cornish hens, also called game hens, are hybrids of small chickens. They weigh from 1 to 1½ pounds and are sold whole or split. Their tender, juicy meat makes Cornish hens excellent for roasting and grilling.

Right:
French Pan-Roasted Hens

Wish-Bone® Marinade Italiano

¾ cup WISH-BONE® Italian Dressing, divided*
2½ to 3 pounds chicken pieces

*Also terrific with Wish-Bone® Robusto Italian or just 2 Good Italian Dressing.

In large, shallow nonaluminum baking dish or plastic bag, pour ½ cup Italian dressing over chicken. Cover, or close bag, and marinate in refrigerator, turning occasionally, 3 to 24 hours.

Remove chicken from marinade; discard marinade. Grill or broil chicken, turning once and brushing frequently with remaining dressing, until chicken is no longer pink in center.   *Makes about 4 servings*

Onion Crumb Chicken Cutlets
Prep Time: 15 *minutes*   **Cook Time:** 4 *to 8 minutes*

1 ⅓ cups French's® Taste Toppers™ French Fried Onions
4 thinly sliced chicken cutlets (1 pound), pounded to ¼-inch thickness
3 tablespoons French's® Hearty Deli Brown Mustard
1 to 2 tablespoons vegetable oil
Salt and pepper to taste

Place **Taste Toppers** in resealable plastic food storage bag; seal. Press with rolling pin until **Taste Toppers** are finely crushed. Transfer to sheet of waxed paper.

Brush each side of chicken with about 1 teaspoon mustard. Dip into **Taste Toppers** crumbs, pressing gently to coat.

Heat 1 tablespoon oil in large nonstick skillet over medium heat. Cook chicken in batches, 1 to 2 minutes per side or until no longer pink in center. Repeat with remaining oil and cutlets. Season to taste with salt and pepper.

Makes 4 servings

Right:
Wish-Bone®
Marinade Italiano

Parmesan Chicken Breasts

Prep Time: 10 *minutes*   **Bake Time:** 25 *minutes*

½ cup KRAFT® 100% Grated Parmesan Cheese
¼ cup dry bread crumbs
 1 teaspoon *each* dried oregano leaves and parsley flakes
¼ teaspoon *each* paprika, salt and black pepper
 6 boneless skinless chicken breast halves (about 2 pounds)
 2 tablespoons butter or margarine, melted

MIX cheese, crumbs and seasonings.

DIP chicken in butter; coat with cheese mixture. Place in 15×10×1-inch baking pan sprayed with no stick cooking spray.

BAKE at 400°F for 20 to 25 minutes or until chicken is no longer pink in center.

Makes 6 servings

Spicy: Substitute ⅛ to ¼ teaspoon ground red pepper for black pepper.

Above:
*Parmesan Chicken
Breasts*

Oven Glazed Chicken

Prep Time: 5 *minutes*   **Cook Time:** 45 *minutes*

 3 pounds chicken, cut into eighths
½ cup *French's*® Honey Mustard Grill & Glaze Sauce or Teriyaki Grill & Glaze Sauce

1. Preheat oven to 350°F. Place chicken in lightly greased baking dish. Brush evenly with **Grill & Glaze** Sauce.

2. Bake 45 minutes or until chicken is no longer pink near bone. Serve with extra **Grill & Glaze** Sauce for dipping.

Makes 4 to 6 servings

Country Chicken Pot Pie

Prep Time: 5 *minutes*   **Cook Time:** 15 *minutes*

    1 package (1.8 ounces) white sauce mix
2¼ cups milk
    2 to 3 cups diced cooked chicken*
    3 cups BIRDS EYE® frozen Mixed Vegetables
1½ cups seasoned croutons**

No leftover cooked chicken handy? Before beginning recipe, cut 1 pound boneless skinless chicken into 1-inch cubes. Cook chicken in 1 tablespoon butter or margarine in large skillet until no longer pink, then proceed with recipe.

**For a quick homemade touch, substitute 4 bakery-bought biscuits for croutons. Split and add to skillet, cut side down.*

• Prepare white sauce mix with milk in large skillet according to package directions.

• Add chicken and vegetables. Bring to boil over medium-high heat; cook 3 minutes or until heated through, stirring occasionally.

• Top with croutons; cover and let stand 5 minutes.   *Makes about 4 servings*

Serving Suggestion: Serve with a green salad.

Plum Paradise Chicken

  1 (3-pound) broiler-fryer chicken, quartered
$\frac{1}{4}$ pound fresh ripe plums, peeled, pitted and coursely chopped
$\frac{1}{2}$ cup KIKKOMAN® Teriyaki Baste & Glaze
  1 tablespoon packed brown sugar

Rinse chicken under cold water; pat dry with paper towels. Place plums in blender or food processor container. Cover; process plums on low speed until smooth. Combine plums with teriyaki baste & glaze and brown sugar; set aside.

Place chicken on grill 5 to 7 inches from medium-hot coals; cook 20 minutes, turning over occasionally. Brush chicken with baste & glaze mixture; cook 10 to 15 minutes longer, or until chicken is no longer pink in center, turning over and brushing frequently with remaining baste & glaze mixture. (Or, place chicken on rack of broiler pan. Broil 5 to 7 inches from heat 15 minutes, turning over occasionally. Brush with baste & glaze mixture; cook 15 minutes longer, or until chicken is no longer pink in center, turning over and brushing frequently with remaining baste & glaze mixture.) *Makes 4 servings*

Above:
*Honey 'n' Spice
Chicken Kabobs*

Honey 'n' Spice Chicken Kabobs

  1 medium green bell pepper, cut into 1-inch squares
  2 boneless skinless chicken breasts, halved (about 1 $\frac{1}{4}$ pounds)
  1 can (8 ounces) pineapple chunks, drained
$\frac{1}{2}$ cup HEINZ® 57 Sauce
$\frac{1}{4}$ cup honey

In small saucepan, blanch bell pepper in boiling water 1 minute; drain. Cut each chicken breast half into 4 pieces. Alternately thread chicken, bell pepper and pineapple onto skewers. In small bowl, combine 57 Sauce and honey. Brush kabobs with 57 Sauce mixture. Grill or broil kabobs, about 6 inches from heat, 12 to 14 minutes or until chicken is tender and no longer pink in center, turning and brushing with 57 Sauce mixture once. *Makes 4 servings*

Pace® Texas Two-Step Chicken Picante

Prep Time: 5 minutes   **Cook Time:** 20 minutes

   4 skinless, boneless chicken breast halves
1 ½ cups PACE® Picante Sauce *or* Thick & Chunky Salsa
   3 tablespoons packed light brown sugar
   1 tablespoon Dijon-style mustard

1. Place chicken in 2-quart shallow baking dish. Mix picante sauce, sugar and mustard. Pour over chicken.

2. Bake at 400°F. for 20 minutes or until chicken is no longer pink in center. Serve with hot cooked rice if desired.

Makes 4 servings

Herb Batter Baked Chicken

⅔ cup prepared HIDDEN VALLEY® Original Ranch® salad dressing
  1 egg, lightly beaten
  1 broiler-fryer chicken (about 3 pounds), cut up
½ cup all-purpose flour
  2 cups cornflake crumbs

Preheat oven to 350°F. On shallow plate, combine salad dressing and egg; set aside. Rinse chicken; pat dry with paper towels. Roll chicken pieces in flour; dip into dressing mixture. Roll in cornflake crumbs. Place chicken on large foil-lined baking pan. Bake until tender and no longer pink, 45 to 50 minutes.

Makes 4 servings

Smart Tip

Brown sugar, a mixture of granulated sugar and molasses, should be moist and clingy when fresh, but it can easily dry out. Adding a slice of apple or bread to the box or bag will restore moisture.

Spiced Turkey with Fruit Salsa

6 ounces turkey breast tenderloin
2 teaspoons lime juice
1 teaspoon mesquite chicken seasoning blend or ground cumin
¼ cup chunky salsa
½ cup frozen pitted sweet cherries, thawed and cut into halves*

*Drained canned sweet cherries may be substituted for frozen cherries.

1. Prepare grill for direct grilling. Brush both sides of turkey with lime juice. Sprinkle both sides with mesquite seasoning.

2. Grill turkey over medium coals 15 to 20 minutes or until turkey is no longer pink in center and juices run clear, turning once.

3. Meanwhile, stir together salsa and cherries in small bowl.

4. Thinly slice turkey. Spoon salsa mixture over turkey.   *Makes 2 servings*

Teriyaki Turkey Burgers

1 pound ground turkey
⅓ cup LAWRY'S® Teriyaki Marinade with Pineapple Juice
3 tablespoons thinly sliced green onions
¼ cup crushed pineapple, drained
½ teaspoon LAWRY'S® Garlic Powder with Parsley

In medium bowl, combine all ingredients; mix well. Form into 4 patties (mixture will be moist). Grill or broil 5 inches from heat source 3 to 5 minutes on each side or until no longer pink in center.   *Makes 4 servings*

Serving Tip

Turkey burgers, like hamburgers, are excellent when served on onion buns with lettuce topped with slices of red onion and pineapple.

Right:
Spiced Turkey with Fruit Salsa

Dad's Favorite Turkey Kabobs

3 ears corn, cut into 1-inch pieces
2 medium zucchini, cut into ¾-inch pieces
2 red bell peppers, cut into 1-inch cubes
2 turkey tenderloins (about 1 pound), cut into 1-inch cubes
⅓ cup reduced-calorie Italian salad dressing
   Additional reduced-calorie Italian salad dressing

In medium saucepan over high heat, blanch corn in boiling water about 1 to 2 minutes. Remove corn from saucepan and plunge into cold water.

In large glass bowl, place corn, zucchini, peppers, turkey and ⅓ cup dressing; cover and refrigerate 1 to 2 hours.

Drain turkey and vegetables, discarding marinade. Alternately thread turkey cubes and vegetables on 8 skewers, leaving ½-inch space between turkey and vegetables.

On outdoor charcoal grill, cook kabobs 18 to 20 minutes, brushing with additional dressing. Turn skewers after first 10 minutes.

Makes 4 servings (8 kabobs)

Favorite recipe from **National Turkey Federation**

Raspberry-Glazed Turkey

½ cup SMUCKER'S® Seedless Red Raspberry Jam
6 tablespoons raspberry vinegar
¼ cup Dijon mustard
4 small turkey breast tenderloins

In large saucepan, stir together jam, vinegar and mustard. Bring to a boil over high heat; cook and stir 3 minutes. Reserve about ½ cup of glaze; coat turkey with some of remaining glaze.

Set turkey on rack in broiler pan. Broil about 4 inches from heat for 15 to 20 minutes or until no longer pink in center, turning and basting once with remaining glaze. Slice turkey crosswise. Serve with reserved glaze.

Makes 4 to 6 servings

Smoked Turkey with Summer Cranberry Nectar

Prep Time: 15 *minutes*

1 BUTTERBALL® Fully Cooked Smoked Young Turkey, thawed, sliced thin
1 can (16 ounces) whole berry cranberry sauce
Juice of ½ lime
1 tablespoon seeded and chopped jalapeño pepper
½ teaspoon salt

Combine cranberry sauce, lime juice, jalapeño pepper and salt in food processor; process until smooth. Spoon cranberry nectar over sliced turkey. Serve with cranberry-studded mini-corn muffins, if desired.

Makes 6 servings

Smart Tip

Jalapeño peppers are small, dark green chilies, normally 2 to 3 inches long and about ¾ inch wide with a blunt or slightly tapered end. Their flavor varies from hot to very hot. They are sold fresh, canned or pickled.

Herb Roasted Turkey

Prep Time: *20 minutes*   **Cook Time:** *3 hours and 30 minutes*
Cool Time: *15 minutes*   **Total Time:** *4 hours and 5 minutes*

1 (12-pound) turkey, thawed if frozen
½ cup FLEISCHMANN'S® Original Margarine, softened and divided
1 tablespoon Italian seasoning

1. Remove neck and giblets from turkey cavities. Rinse turkey; drain well and pat dry. Free legs from tucked position; do not cut band of skin. Using rubber spatula or hand, loosen skin over breast, starting at body cavity opening by legs.

2. Blend 6 tablespoons margarine and Italian seasoning. Spread 2 tablespoons herb mixture inside body cavity; spread remaining herb mixture on meat under skin. Hold skin in place at opening with wooden picks. Return legs to tucked position; turn wings back to hold neck skin in place.

3. Place turkey, breast side up, on flat rack in shallow open pan. Insert meat thermometer deep into thickest part of thigh next to body, not touching bone. Melt remaining 2 tablespoons margarine; brush over skin.

4. Roast at 325°F for 3½ to 3¾ hours. When skin is golden brown, shield breast loosely with foil to prevent overbrowning. Check for doneness; thigh temperature should be 180° to 185°F. Transfer turkey to cutting board and let stand 15 to 20 minutes. Remove wooden picks just before carving.   *Makes 12 servings*

Right:
*Herb Roasted
Turkey*

Maple-Glazed Turkey Breast

1 **bone-in turkey breast (5 to 6 pounds)**
¼ **cup pure maple syrup**
2 **tablespoons butter or margarine, melted**
1 **tablespoon bourbon (optional)**
2 **teaspoons freshly grated orange peel**
   Fresh bay leaves for garnish

1. Prepare barbecue grill with rectangular foil drip pan. Bank briquets on either side of drip pan for indirect cooking.

2. Insert meat thermometer into center of thickest part of turkey breast, not touching bone. Place turkey, bone side down, on roasting rack or directly on grid, directly over drip pan. Grill turkey, on covered grill, over medium coals 55 minutes, adding 4 to 9 briquets to both sides of fire after 45 minutes to maintain medium coals.

3. Combine maple syrup, butter, bourbon and orange peel in small bowl; brush half of mixture over turkey. Continue to grill, covered, 10 minutes. Brush with remaining mixture; continue to grill, covered, about 10 minutes or until thermometer registers 170°F.

4. Transfer turkey to carving board; tent with foil. Let stand 10 minutes before carving. Cut turkey into thin slices. Garnish, if desired.   *Makes 6 to 8 servings*

Variation: For hickory-smoked flavor, cover 2 cups hickory chips with cold water; soak 20 minutes. Drain; sprinkle over coals just before placing turkey on grid.

Quick Tip

Grill-cleaning utensils such as wire brushes and steel wool pads make cleanup after grilling much easier.

Right:
Maple-Glazed Turkey Breast

Roast Turkey with Honey Cranberry Relish

  1 medium orange
12 ounces fresh or frozen whole cranberries
¾ cup honey
  2 pounds sliced roasted turkey breast

Quarter and slice unpeeled orange, removing seeds. Coarsely chop orange and cranberries. Place in medium saucepan and stir in honey. Bring to a boil over medium-high heat. Cook 3 to 4 minutes; cool. Serve over turkey.

Makes 8 servings

Favorite recipe from **National Honey Board**

Above:
Roast Turkey with Honey Cranberry Relish

Italian Turkey Kebabs

Prep Time: *6 to 8 minutes*   **Cook Time:** *15 to 20 minutes*

1 package (about 1 pound) PERDUE® Fresh Sundried Tomato with Garlic
   and Romano Cheese Seasoned Turkey Breast Tenderloins
1 clove garlic, peeled and smashed
1 tablespoon olive oil
1 medium zucchini, cut into chunks
2 bell peppers (1 red and 1 yellow), seeded and cut into chunks
1 yellow onion, peeled and cut into chunks

Prepare outdoor grill for cooking or preheat broiler. Cut turkey into large chunks. In large bowl, combine garlic and oil. Add zucchini, peppers and onion; toss well. Let stand 5 to 10 minutes, tossing occasionally.

Thread turkey pieces on skewers, alternating with zucchini, peppers and onion. Grill or broil kebabs 6 to 8 inches from heat source 15 to 20 minutes, or until turkey is cooked through and vegetables are tender-crisp, turning frequently.

Makes 4 servings

Quick Turkey 'n' Stuffing

Prep Time: *15 minutes*   **Cook Time:** *40 to 45 minutes*

1 package (about 1⅓ pounds) PERDUE® FIT 'N EASY® Fresh Skinless &
   Boneless Turkey Breast
1¼ teaspoons poultry seasoning
   Salt and ground pepper to taste
6 tablespoons butter or margarine, divided
½ cup chopped onion
1 package (6 ounces) stuffing mix for turkey or chicken

With a sharp knife, cut a deep pocket in side of breast. Rub all over with poultry seasoning, salt and pepper. In large, nonstick skillet over medium heat, melt 4 tablespoons butter. Add onion and sauté 2 to 3 minutes, until softened. Prepare stuffing mix following package directions, adding onion and butter mixture.

Preheat oven to 350°F. Stuff breast and secure with toothpicks. Place any remaining stuffing in a greased, shallow roasting pan; place breast on top. Dot top of breast with remaining 2 tablespoons butter. Bake 35 to 45 minutes, until turkey is lightly browned and meat thermometer inserted in thickest part registers 170°F. To serve, remove toothpicks and slice turkey.   *Makes 4 servings*

Seafood

Once an occasional part of our diets, seafood has become more popular due to its greater availability, easy preparation and health benefits. These simple-but-fantastic fish and shellfish recipes will impress your family or guests and have them asking for more.

Right:
Blackened Catfish
(recipe on
page 117)

Dilled Salmon in Parchment

Prep and Cook Time: *20 minutes*

2 skinless salmon fillets (4 to 6 ounces each)
2 tablespoons butter or margarine, melted
1 tablespoon lemon juice
1 tablespoon chopped fresh dill
1 tablespoon chopped shallots
   Salt and pepper

1. Preheat oven to 400°F. Cut 2 pieces parchment paper into 12-inch squares; fold squares in half diagonally and cut into half-heart shapes. Open parchment; place fish fillet on one side of each heart.

2. Combine butter and lemon juice in small cup; drizzle over fish. Sprinkle with dill, shallots, and salt and pepper to taste.

3. Fold parchment hearts in half. Beginning at top of heart, fold edges together, 2 inches at a time. At tip of heart, fold parchment over to seal.

4. Bake fish about 10 minutes or until parchment pouch puffs up. To serve, cut an "X" through top layer of parchment, avoiding hot steam, and fold back points to display contents.

Makes 2 servings

Smart Tip

Seafood, meat or poultry cooked in parchment paper or foil requires little added liquid because the steam created by heating the food creates a moist, tasty final product.

Right:
Dilled Salmon in Parchment

Grilled Swordfish

1 tablespoon lime juice
2 cloves garlic, minced
4 swordfish steaks (5 ounces each)
½ teaspoon chili powder or black pepper
Pineapple Salsa (optional, page 188)

1. Combine lime juice and garlic on plate. Dip swordfish in juice; sprinkle both sides with chili powder.

2. Spray cold grid with nonstick cooking spray. Adjust grid 4 to 6 inches above heat source. Preheat grill to medium-high heat. Grill fish, covered, 2 to 3 minutes. Turn over; grill 1 to 2 minutes more or until just opaque in center and still very moist. Top each serving with about 3 tablespoons Pineapple Salsa, if desired.   *Makes 4 servings*

A.1.® Grilled Fish Steaks

1 pound salmon steaks or other fish steaks, about 1 inch thick
¼ cup A.1.® Steak Sauce
1 tablespoon margarine or butter, melted
½ teaspoon garlic powder

Coat large sheet of aluminum foil with nonstick cooking spray; place fish steaks on foil. In small bowl, combine steak sauce, margarine and garlic powder; spoon over fish. Fold edges of foil together to seal; place seam side up on grill. Grill for about 10 minutes or until fish flakes easily when tested with fork. Carefully remove from grill. Serve immediately.   *Makes 4 servings*

Smart Tip

Fish cooks quickly. Be careful not to overcook it or it will become tough and lose flavor.

Right:
Grilled Swordfish

Fish Broccoli Casserole

1 package (10 ounces) frozen broccoli spears, thawed and drained
1 cup cooked, flaked Florida whitefish
1 can (10¾ ounces) condensed cream of mushroom soup
½ cup milk
¼ teaspoon salt
⅛ teaspoon freshly ground black pepper
½ cup crushed potato chips

Preheat oven to 425°F. Grease 1½-quart casserole. Layer broccoli in prepared casserole. Combine fish, soup, milk, salt and pepper in large bowl.

Spread fish mixture over broccoli. Sprinkle with potato chips. Bake 12 to 15 minutes or until golden brown.   *Makes 4 servings*

Favorite recipe from **Florida Department of Agriculture and Consumer Services, Bureau of Seafood and Aquaculture**

Above:
*Fish Broccoli
Casserole*

Grilled Fresh Fish

3 to 3½ pounds fresh tuna or catfish
¾ cup prepared HIDDEN VALLEY® Original Ranch® Salad Dressing
   Chopped fresh dill
   Lemon wedges (optional)

Place fish on heavy-duty foil. Cover with salad dressing. Grill over medium-hot coals 20 to 30 minutes or until fish turns opaque and flakes easily when tested with fork. Or, broil fish 15 to 20 minutes. Sprinkle with dill; garnish with lemon wedges, if desired.   *Makes 6 servings*

Blackened Catfish

4 (4-ounce) catfish fillets
3 teaspoons lemon juice
   Nonstick garlic-flavored cooking spray
2 teaspoons blackened or Cajun seasoning blend
   Easy Tartar Sauce (optional, page 184)
   Hot cooked rice (optional)

1. Rinse catfish under cold running water; pat dry with paper towel. Sprinkle fillets with 2 teaspoons lemon juice; coat with cooking spray. Sprinkle with seasoning blend; coat again with cooking spray.

2. Heat large nonstick skillet over medium-high heat until hot. Add 2 fillets to skillet, seasoned side down. Cook 3 minutes. Reduce heat to medium and cook 3 minutes more or until fish begins to flake when tested with a fork. Remove fillets from skillet; keep warm. Repeat with remaining fillets. Serve with Easy Tartar Sauce and rice, if desired. *Makes 4 servings*

Smart Tip

Raw fish fillets and steaks should have moist flesh that is free from discoloration and skin that is shiny and resilient. If the fillet or steak has a strong odor, it is not fresh.

Trout Stuffed with Fresh Mint and Oranges

2 pan-dressed* trout (1 to 1¼ pounds each)
½ teaspoon coarse salt, such as Kosher salt
1 orange, sliced
1 cup fresh mint leaves
1 sweet onion, sliced

*A pan-dressed trout has been gutted and scaled with head and tail removed.

1. Rinse trout under cold running water; pat dry with paper towels.

2. Sprinkle cavities of trout with salt; fill each with orange slices and mint. Cover each fish with onion slices.

3. Spray 2 large sheets of foil with nonstick cooking spray. Place 1 fish on each sheet and seal using drugstore wrap technique.**

4. Place foil packets, seam side down, directly on medium-hot coals; grill on covered grill 20 to 25 minutes or until trout flakes easily when tested with fork, turning once.

5. Carefully open foil packets, avoiding hot steam; remove and discard orange-mint stuffing and trout skin. Serve immediately.   *Makes 6 servings*

**Place food in the center of an oblong piece of heavy-duty foil, leaving at least a 2-inch border around the food. Bring the 2 long sides together above the food; fold down in a series of locked folds, allowing for heat circulation and expansion. Fold short ends up and over again. Press folds firmly to seal the foil packet.

Smart Tip

Rinsing fish thoroughly but gently under cold running water removes loose scales and bone fragments.

Right:
Trout Stuffed with Fresh Mint and Oranges

Fish Creole

Prep Time: 5 *minutes*　　**Cook Time:** 20 *minutes*

　　1 **pound fresh or thawed frozen snapper or sole fillets**
　　1 **bag (16 ounces) BIRDS EYE® frozen Farm Fresh Mixtures Broccoli,**
　　　　Green Beans, Pearl Onions & Red Peppers
　　1 **can (16 ounces) tomato sauce**
　　1 **tablespoon dried oregano or Italian seasoning**
　　1 **tablespoon vegetable oil**
　1½ **teaspoons salt**

- Preheat oven to 350°F.

- Place fish in 13×9-inch baking pan.

- In large bowl, combine vegetables, tomato sauce, oregano, oil and salt.

- Pour vegetable mixture over fish.

- Bake 20 minutes or until fish flakes easily when tested with fork.

Makes 4 servings

Savory Baked Fish

　　6 **(8-ounce) scrod, flounder or other boneless mild fish fillets**
　¾ **cup HIDDEN VALLEY® Original Ranch® Dressing**

Preheat oven to 375°F. Arrange fillets in a large, oiled baking pan; spread
2 tablespoons dressing onto each fillet. Bake fish for 10 to 20 minutes,
depending on thickness, or until fish flakes easily when tested with fork. Finish
under broiler to brown top. Serve on julienned vegetables, if desired.

Makes 6 servings

Smart Tip

After handling fish, remove the odor from your hands by rubbing them with salt, then washing them with cold water.

Right:
Fish Creole

Crusty Hot Pan-Fried Fish

1 ½ cups all-purpose flour
3 ½ teaspoons CHEF PAUL PRUDHOMME'S Seafood Magic®, divided
  1 large egg, beaten
  1 cup milk
  6 fish fillets (4 ounces each), speckled trout or drum or your favorite fish
  Vegetable oil for frying

In flat pan, combine flour and 2 teaspoons of the Seafood Magic. In separate pan, combine egg and milk until well blended. Season fillets by sprinkling about ¼ teaspoon of the Seafood Magic on each. In large skillet, heat about ¼ inch oil over medium heat until hot. Meanwhile, coat each fillet with seasoned flour, shake off excess and coat well with milk mixture; then, just before frying, coat fillets once more with flour, shaking off excess. Fry fillets in hot oil until golden brown, 1 to 2 minutes per side. Drain on paper towels and serve immediately on heated serving plates. *Makes 6 servings*

Above:
Crusty Hot Pan-Fried Fish

Grilled Lemon-Teriyaki Fish Steaks

⅓ cup KIKKOMAN® Teriyaki Baste & Glaze
¾ teaspoon grated lemon peel
  2 tablespoons lemon juice
¾ teaspoon dried basil leaves, crumbled
  2 pounds fish steaks (halibut, bass, swordfish or salmon), 1 inch thick

Combine teriyaki baste & glaze, lemon peel, lemon juice and basil. Place fish on oiled grill 4 to 6 inches from hot coals; brush generously with baste & glaze mixture. Cook 4 minutes; turn over. Brush with baste & glaze mixture. Cook 4 minutes longer, or until fish flakes easily with fork, brushing occasionally with remaining baste & glaze mixture. (Or, place fish on rack of broiler pan; brush with baste & glaze mixture. Broil 4 to 5 inches from heat 4 minutes; turn over. Brush with remaining baste & glaze mixture. Broil 4 to 5 minutes longer, or until fish flakes easily when tested with fork.) *Makes 4 servings*

Mustard-Grilled Red Snapper

½ cup Dijon mustard
1 tablespoon red wine vinegar
1 teaspoon ground red pepper
4 red snapper fillets (about 6 ounces each)
Fresh parsley sprigs and red peppercorns (optional)

Spray grid with nonstick cooking spray. Prepare grill for direct cooking.

Combine mustard, vinegar and red pepper in small bowl; mix well. Coat fish thoroughly with mustard mixture.

Place fish on grid. Grill, covered, over medium-high heat 8 minutes or until fish flakes easily when tested with fork, turning halfway through grilling time. Garnish with parsley sprigs and red peppercorns, if desired. *Makes 4 servings*

Below:
*Mustard-Grilled
Red Snapper*

Broiled Orange Roughy with Green Peppercorn Sauce

1 cup loosely packed cilantro leaves
2 tablespoons Dijon mustard
2 tablespoons dry white wine
½ teaspoon green peppercorns, rinsed and drained
4 orange roughy fillets (about 6 ounces each)

1. Preheat broiler. Position oven rack about 4 inches from heat source.

2. Combine all ingredients except fish in food processor or blender container; process until well blended. Set aside.

3. Place fish in shallow baking pan; top with sauce.

4. Broil 10 minutes or until fish flakes easily when tested with fork.

Makes 4 servings

Flounder Fillets with Carrots

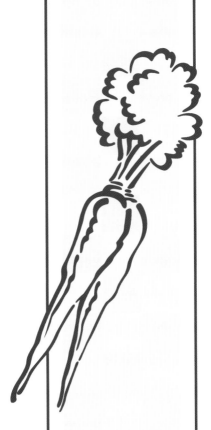

  1 **pound carrots, julienned (about 4 large)**
  2 **tablespoons minced parsley**
  1 **teaspoon olive oil**
$\frac{1}{8}$ **teaspoon salt**
$\frac{1}{8}$ **teaspoon pepper**
  4 **(4 to 5 ounces each) flounder fillets***
  2 **teaspoons coarse-grain Dijon mustard**
  1 **teaspoon honey**

*Or, substitute other fish fillets, such as tilapia, sole, cod, catfish, halibut, ocean perch, trout, orange roughy or pollock.

Microwave Directions: Combine carrots, parsley, oil, salt and pepper in 11×7-inch microwavable baking dish. Cover with waxed paper. Microwave at HIGH 5 minutes, stirring once.

Fold thin fillets in half to give all fillets even thickness. Place fillets over carrots with thick parts toward corners of dish. Combine mustard and honey; spread over fillets.

Cover with waxed paper. Microwave at HIGH 2 minutes. Rotate fillets, placing cooked parts toward center; continue to cook 1 to 3 minutes longer or just until fish flakes easily when tested with a fork. Let stand, covered, 2 minutes. Serve fish and carrots on warm plates. *Makes 4 servings*

Favorite recipe from **National Fisheries Institute**

Right:
*Flounder Fillet
with Carrots*

Salmon on a Bed of Leeks

3 to 4 leeks
2 teaspoons butter or margarine
½ cup dry white wine or vermouth
2 salmon fillets (6 to 8 ounces)
Salt and black pepper to taste
2 tablespoons grated Gruyère cheese

Cut off roots and top inch of green ends from leeks; discard. Cut leeks lengthwise into quarters, leaving ⅓ inch together at root end. Separate sections and rinse thoroughly under cold running water; drain well. Separate at root end.

In 10-inch skillet, melt butter over medium heat. Add leeks; cook 2 to 3 minutes, stirring often, until leeks are wilted. Stir in wine; arrange salmon on leeks. Sprinkle with salt and pepper. Reduce heat to low. Cover; cook 5 minutes. Sprinkle cheese over salmon. Cover; cook another 3 to 5 minutes or until salmon is firm and opaque around edges and cheese is melted. Transfer to warm dinner plate using broad spatula; serve immediately. *Makes 2 servings*

Favorite recipe from **National Fisheries Institute**

Smart Tip

Salmon has a higher fat content than most fish, but its fat content is made up primarily of nutritious omega-3 fatty acids. Research indicates that omega-3 may lower the risk of heart attack and heart disease.

Right:
Salmon on a Bed of Leeks

Red Snapper with Lime-Ginger Butter

Prep and Cook Time: *18 minutes*

5 tablespoons butter, cut into small pieces
1 tablespoon lime juice
3 cloves garlic
2 teaspoons ground ginger
$\frac{1}{2}$ teaspoon hot pepper sauce
   Salt
   Black pepper
6 red snapper fillets (about 1 $\frac{1}{2}$ pounds)

1. Preheat broiler.

2. Combine butter, lime juice, garlic, ginger, pepper sauce, and salt and pepper to taste in food processor; process until smooth paste forms.

3. Broil red snapper 4 to 5 inches from heat 5 minutes. Turn fillets over and broil 4 minutes.

4. Place about 1 tablespoon butter mixture on top of each fillet; broil 45 seconds. Serve immediately.

Makes 6 servings

Tip: Halibut or swordfish can be substituted for the red snapper.

Serving Tip

For a special touch, serve fish with rice and garnish with fresh lime slices and chives.

Right:
Red Snapper with Lime-Ginger Butter

Shanghai Steamed Fish

1 cleaned whole sea bass, red snapper, carp or grouper
   (about 1 ½ pounds)
¼ cup teriyaki sauce
2 teaspoons grated fresh ginger
2 green onions, cut into 4-inch pieces
1 teaspoon dark sesame oil (optional)
   Bell pepper strips (optional)
   Green onions (optional)

1. Sprinkle inside cavity of fish with teriyaki sauce and ginger. Place onions in cavity in single layer.

2. Place steaming rack in wok. Pour enough water into wok so that water is just below steaming rack. Bring water to a boil in wok. Reduce heat to medium-low to maintain a simmer. Place fish on steaming rack in wok. Cover and steam fish over simmering water about 10 minutes per inch of thickness measured at thickest part. Fish is done when it flakes easily when tested with fork.

3. Carefully remove fish; discard onions. Cut fish into 4 serving-size portions. Sprinkle with sesame oil, if desired. Garnish with pepper strips and green onions, if desired.

Makes 4 servings

Serving Tip

Cooks are serving more fish than ever before, since it is versatile, delicious and nutritious . . . and cooks quickly.

Right:
Shanghai Steamed Fish

Nutty Pan-Fried Trout

2 tablespoons oil
4 trout fillets (about 6 ounces each)
¹/₂ cup seasoned bread crumbs
¹/₂ cup pine nuts

1. Heat oil in large skillet over medium heat. Lightly coat fish with crumbs. Add to skillet.

2. Cook 8 minutes or until fish flakes easily when tested with fork, turning after 5 minutes. Remove fish from skillet. Place on serving platter; keep warm.

3. Add nuts to drippings in skillet. Cook and stir 3 minutes or until nuts are lightly toasted. Sprinkle over fish.   *Makes 4 servings*

Snapper Pouches with Ginger and Lime

4 red snapper or halibut fillets (about 5 ounces each)
8 tablespoons finely chopped red bell pepper
Pinch each salt and ground black pepper
4 tablespoons I CAN'T BELIEVE IT'S NOT BUTTER!® Spread
8 teaspoons lime juice
2 teaspoons chopped fresh ginger *or* ¹/₂ teaspoon ground ginger

Preheat oven to 400°F. On four 12×18-inch pieces of heavy-duty aluminum foil, place 1 fillet skin side down, then sprinkle each with 2 tablespoons bell pepper. Season each with salt and pepper. Evenly top with 4 tablespoons I Can't Believe It's Not Butter! Spread, lime juice and ginger. Fold foil, sealing edges airtight with double-fold.

On large baking sheet, arrange pouches. Bake 25 minutes or until fish flakes easily when tested with fork.   *Makes 4 servings*

Above:
*Nutty Pan-Fried
Trout*

Swanson® Quick 'n' Easy Salmon

Prep Time: 5 *minutes* **Cook Time:** 15 *minutes*

- 1 can (14½ ounces) SWANSON® Chicken Broth (1¾ cups)
- ¼ cup Chablis *or* other dry white wine
- ¼ teaspoon dried dill weed, crushed
- 4 thin lemon slices
- 4 salmon steaks, 1 inch thick (about 1½ pounds)

1. In medium skillet mix broth, wine, dill and lemon. Over medium-high heat, heat to a boil.

2. Place fish in broth mixture. Reduce heat to low. Cover and cook 10 minutes or until fish flakes easily when tested with fork. Discard poaching liquid.

Makes 4 servings

Below:
Swanson® Quick 'n' Easy Salmon

Grilled Swordfish Steaks

- 1 cup uncooked UNCLE BEN'S® CONVERTED® Brand Rice
- 4 (1-inch-thick) swordfish steaks (about 4 ounces each)
- 3 tablespoons Caribbean jerk seasoning
- 1 can (8 ounces) crushed pineapple in juices, drained
- ⅓ cup chopped macadamia nuts
- 1 tablespoon honey

1. Cook rice according to package directions.

2. During the last 10 minutes of cooking, coat both sides of swordfish steaks with jerk seasoning. Lightly spray grid of preheated grill with nonstick cooking spray. Grill swordfish over medium coals 10 to 12 minutes or until fish flakes easily when tested with fork, turning after 5 minutes.

3. Stir pineapple, nuts and honey into hot cooked rice; serve with fish.

Makes 4 servings

Smart Tip

For a nuttier flavor, place macadamia nuts in a small nonstick skillet and toast over medium-high heat until lightly browned, stirring occasionally.

Pasta with Tuna Sauce

Prep Time: 5 *minutes*   **Cook Time:** 20 *minutes*

3 cups bow tie pasta, uncooked
1 box (9 ounces) BIRDS EYE® frozen Italian Green Beans
1 jar (15 ounces) prepared spaghetti sauce
1 can (6 ounces) tuna packed in water, drained
Chopped Italian parsley (optional)

• Cook pasta according to package directions; drain.

• Cook vegetables according to package directions; drain.

• Combine pasta, beans, spaghetti sauce, tuna and parsley. Cook and stir over medium-high heat 5 minutes or until heated through.   *Makes about 2 servings*

Jamaican Shrimp & Pineapple Kabobs

Prep and Cook Time: 25 *minutes*

½ cup prepared jerk sauce
¼ cup pineapple preserves
2 tablespoons minced fresh chives
1 pound large shrimp, peeled and deveined
½ medium pineapple, peeled, cored and cut into 1-inch cubes
2 large red, green or yellow bell peppers, cut into 1-inch cubes

1. Combine jerk sauce, preserves and chives in small bowl; mix well. Thread shrimp, pineapple and peppers onto 4 skewers; brush with jerk sauce mixture.

2. Grill kabobs over medium-hot coals 6 to 10 minutes or until shrimp turn pink and opaque, turning once. Serve with remaining jerk sauce mixture. mixture. Serve kabobs with hot cooked rice, if desired.   *Makes 4 servings*

Cutting Corners: Purchase pineapple already trimmed and cored in the produce section of your local supermarket.

Right:
Jamaican Shrimp
& Pineapple
Kabobs

Scallops with Tomatoes and Basil

Prep Time: *10 minutes*   **Cook Time:** *5 minutes*

8 to 12 large sea scallops, halved crosswise if large
   Salt and freshly ground black pepper, to taste
3 tablespoons FLEISCHMANN'S® Original Margarine, divided
2 tomatoes, peeled, seeded and chopped
2 tablespoons chopped fresh or 2 teaspoons dried basil leaves

1. Dry scallops with paper towels; season with salt and pepper.

2. Heat 2 tablespoons margarine in large nonstick skillet over medium-high heat.

3. Arrange half the scallops in a single layer in skillet; cook for 1 to 2 minutes on each side or just until opaque. Transfer scallops to a platter; keep warm. Repeat with remaining scallops; remove to serving platter.

4. Melt remaining margarine in same skillet over medium-high heat. Add tomatoes and basil; heat through.

5. Spoon tomato mixture over scallops; serve immediately.   *Makes 2 servings*

Smart Tip

Shop for scallops that have a fresh appearance, including a moist surface. Fresh scallops should have a sweet smell. Avoid those with a pronounced sulfer odor.

Right:
Scallops with Tomatoes and Basil

Below:
Seafood Risotto

Seafood Risotto

Prep Time: 5 *minutes*   **Cook Time:** 15 *minutes*

1 package (5.2 ounces) rice in creamy sauce (Risotto Milanese flavor)
1 package (14 to 16 ounces) frozen fully cooked shrimp
1 box (10 ounces) BIRDS EYE® frozen Mixed Vegetables
2 teaspoons grated Parmesan cheese

• In 4-quart saucepan, prepare rice according to package directions. Add frozen shrimp and vegetables during last 10 minutes of cooking.

• Sprinkle with cheese. Serve hot.   *Makes 4 servings*

Penne Pasta with Shrimp & Roasted Red Pepper Sauce

12 ounces uncooked penne pasta
1 cup low-sodium chicken or vegetable broth, defatted
1 cup GUILTLESS GOURMET® Roasted Red Pepper Salsa
1 cup chopped fresh or low-sodium canned and drained tomatoes
12 ounces medium raw shrimp, peeled and deveined
   Fresh Italian parsley sprigs (optional)

Cook pasta according to package directions; drain and keep warm.

Meanwhile, combine broth, salsa and tomatoes in 1-quart saucepan. Bring to a boil over medium-high heat. Reduce heat to medium; simmer about 5 minutes or until hot. Allow to cool slightly.

Pour broth mixture into food processor or blender; process until smooth. Return to saucepan; bring back to a simmer. Add shrimp; simmer 2 minutes or just until shrimp turn pink and opaque. D*o not overcook.* To serve, divide pasta among 4 warm serving plates. Cover each serving with sauce, dividing shrimp equally among each serving. Garnish with parsley, if desired.   *Makes 4 servings*

Right:
Penne Pasta with Shrimp & Roasted Red Pepper Sauce

Steamed Maryland Crabs

1 pint water or beer
1 pint cider vinegar or white vinegar
2 dozen live Maryland blue crabs
½ pound seafood seasoning
½ pound salt

1. Place water and vinegar in 10-gallon stockpot. Place rack in bottom of pot. Place half of crabs on rack. Mix seafood seasoning with salt and sprinkle half over crabs.

2. Repeat layering with remaining crabs and seasoning mixture.

3. Cover pot. Heat on high until liquid begins to steam. Steam about 25 minutes or until crabs turn red and meat is white. Remove crabs to large serving platter using tongs.

4. Cover table with disposable paper cloth.

5. To pick crabs, place crab on its back. With thumb or knife point, pry off "apron" flap (the "pull tab"-looking shell in the center) and discard.

6. Lift off top shell and discard.

7. Break off toothed claws and set aside. With knife edge, scrape off 3 areas of lungs and debris over hard semi-transparent membrane covering edible crabmeat.

8. Hold crab at each side; break apart at center. Discard legs. Remove membrane cover with knife, exposing large chunks of meat; remove with fingers or knife.

9. Crack claws with mallet or knife handle to expose meat.   *Makes 4 servings*

Right:
Steamed Maryland Crabs

One-Dish
MEALS

Right:
Asian Chicken and Noodles (recipe on page 146)

S*ave time and hassle—and win fans—with these simple one-dish wonders. Create hearty soups everyone will love, or put together a tasty skillet dish or casserole. Great one-dish meals translate into happy smiles!*

Campbell's® Garlic Mashed Potatoes & Beef Bake

Prep Time: 10 *minutes*   **Cook Time:** 20 *minutes*

1 pound ground beef
1 can (10¾ ounces) CAMPBELL'S® Condensed Cream of Mushroom with
    Roasted Garlic Soup
1 tablespoon Worcestershire sauce
1 bag (16 ounces) frozen vegetable combination (broccoli, cauliflower,
    carrots), thawed
3 cups hot mashed potatoes

1. In medium skillet over medium-high heat, cook beef until browned, stirring to separate meat. Pour off fat.

2. In 2-quart shallow baking dish mix beef, **½ *can*** soup, Worcestershire and vegetables.

3. Stir remaining soup into potatoes. Spoon potato mixture over beef mixture. Bake at 400°F. for 20 minutes or until hot.   *Makes 4 servings*

Easy Ham & Veg•All® Chowder

Prep Time: 7 *minutes*

2 cans (15 ounces each) VEG•ALL® Original Mixed Vegetables, with liquid
1 can (10¾ ounces) cream of potato soup
1 cup cubed cooked ham
½ teaspoon dried basil
¼ teaspoon black pepper

Right:
*Campbell's® Garlic
Mashed Potatoes &
Beef Bake*

In medium saucepan, combine Veg•All, soup, ham, basil and pepper. Heat until hot; serve.   *Makes 4 to 6 servings*

Above:
Cajun Chicken Bayou

Serving Tip

To make this Cajun dish a bit spicier, add hot pepper sauce just before serving.

Cajun Chicken Bayou

2 cups water
1 can (10 ounces) diced tomatoes and green chilies, undrained
1 box UNCLE BEN'S® Red Beans & Rice
2 boneless, skinless chicken breasts (about 8 ounces)

1. In large skillet, combine water, tomatoes, beans & rice and contents of seasoning packet; mix well.

2. Add chicken. Bring to a boil. Cover; reduce heat and simmer 20 minutes or until chicken is no longer pink in center.   *Makes 2 servings*

Asian Chicken and Noodles

Prep Time: 5 *minutes*   **Cook Time:** 20 *minutes*

1 package (3 ounces) chicken flavor instant ramen noodles
1 bag (16 ounces) BIRDS EYE® frozen Farm Fresh Mixtures Broccoli, Carrots and Water Chestnuts*
1 tablespoon vegetable oil
1 pound boneless skinless chicken breasts, cut into thin strips
¼ cup stir-fry sauce

Or, substitute 1 bag (16 ounces) Birds Eye® frozen Broccoli Cuts.

• Reserve seasoning packet from noodles.

• Bring 2 cups water to boil in large saucepan. Add noodles and vegetables. Cook 3 minutes, stirring occasionally; drain.

• Meanwhile, heat oil in large nonstick skillet over medium-high heat. Add chicken; cook and stir until browned, about 8 minutes.

• Stir in noodles, vegetables, stir-fry sauce and reserved seasoning packet; heat through.   *Makes about 4 servings*

Swanson® Quick Vegetable Soup

Prep Time: 10 *minutes*   **Cook Time:** 20 *minutes*

2 cans (14½ ounces *each*) SWANSON® Vegetable Broth
½ teaspoon dried basil leaves, crushed
¼ teaspoon garlic powder
1 can (about 14½ ounces) whole peeled tomatoes, cut up
1 package (about 9 ounces) frozen mixed vegetables (about 2 cups)
1 cup *uncooked* corkscrew macaroni

In medium saucepan mix broth, basil, garlic powder, tomatoes and vegetables. Over medium-high heat, heat to a boil. Stir in macaroni. Reduce heat to medium. Cook 15 minutes or until macaroni is done, stirring occasionally.

Makes 6 servings

Cheesy Beef Stroganoff

Prep Time: 10 *minutes*   **Cook Time:** 15 *minutes*

1 pound ground beef
2 cups water
3 cups (6 ounces) medium egg noodles, uncooked
¾ pound (12 ounces) VELVEETA® Pasteurized Prepared Cheese Product, cut up
1 can (10¾ ounces) condensed cream of mushroom soup
¼ teaspoon black pepper

1. Brown meat in large skillet; drain.

2. Stir in water. Bring to boil. Stir in noodles. Reduce heat to medium-low; cover. Simmer 8 minutes or until noodles are tender.

3. Add Velveeta, soup and pepper; stir until Velveeta is melted.

Makes 4 to 6 servings

Below:
*Cheesy Beef
Stroganoff*

Curried Chicken with Couscous
Prep Time: 5 *minutes*   **Cook Time:** 15 *minutes*

- 1 package (5.7 ounces) curry flavor couscous mix
- 1 tablespoon butter or margarine
- 1 pound boneless, skinless chicken breasts, cut into thin strips
- 1 ½ cups BIRDS EYE® frozen Farm Fresh Mixtures Broccoli, Cauliflower & Red Peppers
- 1 ⅓ cups water
- ½ cup raisins

• Remove seasoning packet from couscous mix; set aside.

• In large nonstick skillet, melt butter over medium-high heat. Add chicken; cook until browned on all sides.

• Stir in vegetables, water, raisins and seasoning packet; bring to boil. Reduce heat to medium-low; cover and simmer 5 minutes or until chicken is no longer pink in center.

• Stir in couscous; cover. Remove from heat; let stand 5 minutes. Stir before serving. *Makes 4 servings*

Serving Suggestion: Serve with toasted pita bread rounds.

Smart Tip

To add flavor to chicken breasts, simply rub them with lemon juice before cooking.

Clam Chowder
Prep Time: 1 *minute*   **Cook Time:** 10 *to* 12 *minutes*

- 1 bag (16 ounces) BIRDS EYE® frozen Small Whole Onions
- 1 can (14 ounces) vegetable broth
- 2 cans (10 ounces each) clam chowder

• In large saucepan, place onions and broth; bring to boil over high heat. Reduce heat to medium; cover and simmer 7 to 10 minutes or until onions are tender.

• Stir in clam chowder; cook until heated through. *Makes 4 servings*

Right:
Curried Chicken with Couscous

Broccoli, Chicken and Rice Casserole

1 box UNCLE BEN'S® Broccoli Rice au Gratin
2 cups boiling water
4 boneless, skinless chicken breasts (about 1 pound)
¼ teaspoon garlic powder
2 cups frozen broccoli
1 cup (4 ounces) reduced-fat shredded Cheddar cheese

1. Heat oven to 425°F. In 13×9-inch baking pan, combine rice and contents of seasoning packet. Add boiling water; mix well. Add chicken; sprinkle with garlic powder. Cover and bake 30 minutes.

2. Add broccoli and cheese; continue to bake, covered, 8 to 10 minutes or until chicken is no longer pink in center. *Makes 4 servings*

Golden Glazed Flank Steak

1 envelope LIPTON® RECIPE SECRETS® Onion Soup Mix*
1 jar (12 ounces) apricot or peach preserves
½ cup water
1 beef flank steak (about 2 pounds), cut into thin strips
2 medium green, red and/or yellow bell peppers, sliced
Hot cooked rice

Also terrific with LIPTON® RECIPE SECRETS® Onion-Mushroom, Garlic Mushroom or Fiesta Herb with Red Pepper Soup Mix.

1. In small bowl, combine soup mix, preserves and water; set aside.

2. On heavy-duty aluminum foil or in bottom of broiler pan with rack removed, arrange steak and peppers; top with soup mixture.

3. Grill or broil, turning steak and vegetables once, until steak is done. Serve over hot rice. *Makes 8 servings*

Right:
Broccoli, Chicken and Rice Casserole

Hearty Minestrone Soup

Prep Time: 10 *minutes*   **Cook Time:** 5 *minutes*

    2 cans (10¾ ounces each) condensed Italian tomato soup
    3 cups water
    3 cups cooked vegetables, such as zucchini, peas, corn or beans
    2 cups cooked ditalini pasta
1 ⅓ cups *French's*® *Taste Toppers*™ French Fried Onions

Combine soup and water in large saucepan. Add vegetables and pasta. Bring to a boil. Reduce heat. Cook until heated through, stirring often.

Place **Taste Toppers** in microwavable dish. Microwave on HIGH 1 minute or until **Taste Toppers** are golden.

Ladle soup into individual bowls. Sprinkle with **Taste Toppers.**   *Makes 6 servings*

Below:
*Campbell's® One-
Dish Chicken
& Rice Bake*

Campbell's® One-Dish Chicken & Rice Bake

Prep Time: 5 *minutes*   **Cook Time:** 45 *minutes*

1 can (10¾ ounces) CAMPBELL'S® Condensed Cream of Mushroom Soup
     or 98% Fat Free Cream of Mushroom Soup
1 cup water*
¾ cup *uncooked* regular white rice
¼ teaspoon paprika
¼ teaspoon pepper
4 skinless, boneless chicken breast halves (about 1 pound)

*For creamier rice, increase water to 1⅓ cups.

1. In 2-quart shallow baking dish mix soup, water, rice, paprika and pepper. Place chicken on rice mixture. Sprinkle with additional paprika and pepper. **Cover.**

2. Bake at 375°F. for 45 minutes or until chicken is no longer pink and rice is done.

Makes 4 servings

Right:
*Hearty Minestrone
Soup*

15 Minute Cheesy Chicken & Vegetable Rice

1 tablespoon oil
4 small boneless skinless chicken breast halves (about 1 pound)
1 can (14½ ounces) chicken broth *or* 1¾ cups water
2 cups MINUTE® White Rice, uncooked
1 package (16 ounces) frozen vegetable blend (such as broccoli, cauliflower and carrots), thawed, drained
¾ pound (12 ounces) VELVEETA® Pasteurized Prepared Cheese Product, cut up

1. Heat oil in large nonstick skillet on medium-high heat. Add chicken; cover. Cook 4 minutes on each side or until cooked through. Remove chicken from skillet.

2. Add broth to skillet. Bring to boil.

3. Stir in rice, vegetables and Velveeta. Top with chicken; cover. Cook on low heat 5 minutes. Stir until Velveeta is melted.   *Makes 4 servings*

Note: Increase oil to 2 tablespoons if using regular skillet.

Chili Stew

Prep Time: *2 minutes*   **Cook Time:** *7 to 10 minutes*

1 box (10 ounces) BIRDS EYE® frozen Sweet Corn
2 cans (15 ounces each) chili
1 can (14 ounces) stewed tomatoes
Chili powder

• In large saucepan, cook corn according to package directions; drain.

• Stir in chili and tomatoes; cook until heated through.

• Stir in chili powder to taste.   *Makes 4 servings*

Serving Tip

Serve this chili stew with your favorite corn bread or sprinkle it with shredded Cheddar cheese.

Right:
15 Minute Cheesy Chicken & Vegetable Rice

Chicken Gumbo

Prep Time: 5 *minutes*   **Cook Time:** 20 *minutes*

3 tablespoons vegetable oil
1 pound boneless skinless chicken breasts, cut into 1-inch pieces
½ pound smoked sausage, cut into ¾-inch slices
1 bag (16 ounces) BIRDS EYE® frozen Farm Fresh Mixtures Broccoli, Corn
   and Red Peppers
1 can (14½ ounces) stewed tomatoes
1½ cups water

• Heat oil in large saucepan over high heat. Add chicken and sausage; cook until browned, about 8 minutes.

• Add vegetables, tomatoes and water; bring to boil. Reduce heat to medium; cover and cook 3 minutes.

Makes 4 to 6 servings

Cheesy Italian Chicken

Prep Time: 5 *minutes*   **Cook Time:** 20 *minutes*

4 boneless skinless chicken breast halves (about 1¼ pounds)
1 can (15 ounces) chunky Italian-style tomato sauce or 1 jar (15 ounces)
   chunky spaghetti sauce
½ pound (8 ounces) VELVEETA® Pasteurized Prepared Cheese Product,
   cut up
Hot cooked pasta

1. Spray large skillet with no stick cooking spray. Add chicken; brown on medium-high heat 1 to 2 minutes on each side. Reduce heat to low.

2. Stir in tomato sauce; cover. Simmer 12 to 15 minutes or until chicken is cooked through.

3. Add Velveeta; cover. Cook on low heat until Velveeta is melted. Serve over pasta.

Makes 4 servings

Right:
Chicken Gumbo

Grilled Vegetables & Brown Rice

1 medium zucchini
1 medium red or yellow bell pepper, quartered lengthwise
1 small onion, cut crosswise into 1-inch-thick slices
¾ cup Italian dressing
4 cups hot cooked UNCLE BEN'S® Brown Rice

1. Cut zucchini lengthwise into thirds. Place all vegetables in large resealable plastic food storage bag; add dressing. Seal bag; refrigerate several hours or overnight.

2. Remove vegetables from marinade, reserving marinade. Place bell peppers and onion on grill over medium coals; brush with marinade. Grill 5 minutes. Turn vegetables over; add zucchini. Brush with marinade. Continue grilling until vegetables are crisp-tender, about 5 minutes, turning zucchini over after 3 minutes.

3. Remove vegetables from grill; coarsely chop. Add to hot rice; mix lightly. Season with salt and black pepper, if desired.   *Makes 6 to 8 servings*

Tip: The easiest way to grill vegetables? Cut them into large pieces, toss them in salad dressing or seasoned oil and place them directly on the grill or in tightly wrapped foil packets.

Above:
*Grilled Vegetables
& Brown Rice*

Shrimp & Asparagus Fettuccine

Prep Time: 5 minutes   **Cook Time:** 20 minutes

12 ounces uncooked fettuccine
1 box (10 ounces) BIRDS EYE® frozen Asparagus Cuts*
1 tablespoon vegetable oil
1 package (16 ounces) frozen, uncooked cocktail-size shrimp
1 jar (12 ounces) prepared alfredo sauce
1 jar (4 ounces) sliced pimientos, drained

Or, substitute 1½ cups Birds Eye® frozen Green Peas or Birds Eye® frozen Broccoli Cuts.

• Cook pasta according to package directions, adding asparagus to water 8 minutes before pasta is done. Drain; keep warm.

• Meanwhile, heat oil in large skillet over medium-high heat. Add shrimp; cover and cook 3 minutes or until shrimp turn pink. Drain excess liquid, leaving shrimp and about 2 tablespoons liquid in skillet. Reduce heat to low. Stir in alfredo sauce and pimiento. Cover; cook 5 minutes. *Do not boil.*

• Toss fettuccine and asparagus with shrimp mixture.   *Makes about 4 servings*

Below:
*Shrimp &
Asparagus
Fettuccine*

Steak & Pepper Fajitas
Prep Time: 10 minutes   **Cook Time:** 5 to 7 minutes

1 packet (1.12 ounces) fajita marinade
1 pound boneless steak,* cut into thin strips
1 bag (16 ounces) BIRDS EYE® frozen Farm Fresh Mixtures Pepper Stir Fry vegetables
8 (6- to 7-inch) flour tortillas, warmed
½ cup salsa

*Or, substitute 1 pound boneless, skinless chicken, cut into strips.

• Prepare fajita marinade according to package directions.

• Add steak and vegetables. Let stand 10 minutes.

• Heat large skillet over medium-high heat. Remove steak and vegetables with slotted spoon and place in skillet.

• Add marinade, if desired. Cook 5 minutes or until steak is desired doneness and mixture is heated through, stirring occasionally.

• Wrap mixture in tortillas. Top with salsa.   Makes 4 servings

Birds Eye® Idea: Vegetables do not have to be fresh to be nutritious. Add cooked Birds Eye® broccoli or spinach to frozen pizza.

Serving Tip

Serve these zesty fajitas with guacamole and sour cream on the side. Or, serve the beef and vegetable mixture over rice if you don't have tortillas on hand.

Right:
Steak & Pepper Fajita

1-2-3 Cheddar Broccoli Casserole

Prep Time: *5 minutes*   **Cook Time:** *20 minutes*

1 jar (16 ounces) RAGÚ® Cheese Creations!® Double Cheddar Sauce
2 boxes (10 ounces each) frozen broccoli florets, thawed
¼ cup plain or Italian seasoned dry bread crumbs
1 tablespoon margarine or butter, melted

1. Preheat oven to 350°F. In 1½-quart casserole, combine Ragú Cheese Creations! Sauce and broccoli.

2. Evenly top with bread crumbs combined with margarine.

3. Bake uncovered 20 minutes or until bread crumbs are golden and broccoli is tender.   *Makes 6 servings*

One-Dish Meal

2 bags SUCCESS® Rice
Vegetable cooking spray
1 cup cubed cooked turkey-ham*
1 cup (4 ounces) shredded low-fat Cheddar cheese
1 cup peas

*Or, use cooked turkey, ham or turkey franks.

Prepare rice according to package directions.

Spray 1-quart microwave-safe dish with cooking spray; set aside. Place rice in medium bowl. Add turkey-ham, cheese and peas; mix lightly. Spoon into prepared dish; smooth into even layer with spoon. Microwave on HIGH 1 minute; stir. Microwave 30 seconds or until thoroughly heated.   *Makes 4 servings*

Conventional Directions: Assemble casserole as directed. Spoon into ovenproof 1-quart baking dish sprayed with vegetable cooking spray. Bake at 350°F until thoroughly heated, about 15 to 20 minutes.

Right:
1-2-3 Cheddar Broccoli Casserole

Above:
Potato-Bacon Soup

Smart Tip

For a quick and easy way to chop bacon, try snipping it with a pair of scissors while it is partially frozen.

Potato-Bacon Soup
Prep and Cook Time: 27 *minutes*

2 cans (about 14 ounces each) chicken broth
3 russet potatoes (1¾ to 2 pounds), peeled and cut into ½-inch cubes
1 medium onion, finely chopped
1 teaspoon dried thyme leaves
4 to 6 strips bacon (4 to 6 ounces), chopped
½ cup (2 ounces) shredded Cheddar cheese

1. Combine broth, potatoes, onion and thyme in Dutch oven; bring to a boil over high heat. Reduce heat to medium-high and boil 10 minutes or until potatoes are tender.

2. While potatoes are cooking, place bacon in microwavable container. Cover with paper towels and cook on HIGH 6 to 7 minutes or until bacon is crisp, stirring after 3 minutes. Break up bacon.

3. Immediately transfer bacon to broth mixture; simmer 3 to 5 minutes. Season to taste with salt and pepper. Ladle into bowls and sprinkle with cheese.

Makes 4 servings

DI GIORNO® Easy Chicken Cacciatore with Light Ravioli
Prep Time: 5 *minutes*　　Cook Time: 10 *minutes*

1 package (9 ounces) DI GIORNO® Light Cheese Ravioli
2 boneless skinless chicken breast halves, cut into strips
1 large green pepper, thinly sliced
1 package (15 ounces) DI GIORNO® Marinara Sauce

PREPARE pasta as directed on package.

MEANWHILE, spray large nonstick skillet with no stick cooking spray. Add chicken; cook and stir on medium-high heat until cooked through. Add green pepper; cook and stir 1 minute.

STIR in sauce; cook on low heat 1 minute or until thoroughly heated. Toss with pasta. Sprinkle with DI GIORNO Shredded Parmesan Cheese, if desired.

Makes 4 servings

Western Wagon Wheels

Prep Time: *5 minutes*   **Cook Time:** *25 minutes*

   1 **pound lean ground beef or ground turkey**
   2 **cups wagon wheel pasta, uncooked**
   1 **can (14 1/2 ounces) stewed tomatoes**
1 1/2 **cups water**
   1 **box (10 ounces) BIRDS EYE® frozen Sweet Corn**
 1/2 **cup barbecue sauce**
     Salt and pepper to taste

• In large skillet, cook beef over medium heat 5 minutes or until well browned.

• Stir in pasta, tomatoes, water, corn and barbecue sauce; bring to a boil.

• Reduce heat to low; cover and simmer 15 to 20 minutes or until pasta is tender, stirring occasionally. Season with salt and pepper.   *Makes 4 servings*

Serving Suggestion: Serve with corn bread or corn muffins.

Below:
*Western Wagon
Wheels*

Right:
*Beef Enchiladas
Olé*

Smart Tip

*Flour tortillas
come in many
colors and
sizes. You'll
find them
in the
refrigerated
dairy case or
grocery aisle
of the
supermarket.*

Beef Enchiladas Olé

Prep Time: *20 minutes*　　　**Microwave Time:** *6 minutes*

1 pound ground beef or 1 pound boneless skinless chicken breasts, chopped
1 cup TACO BELL® HOME ORIGINALS®* Thick 'N Chunky Salsa, divided
**1 pound (16 ounces) VELVEETA® Mexican Pasteurized Process Cheese
Spread with Jalapeño Peppers, cut up, divided**
10 flour tortillas

*TACO BELL and HOME ORIGINALS are registered trademarks owned and licensed by Taco Bell Corp.

1. Brown meat; drain. Stir in ½ cup of the salsa and ½ of the Velveeta; cook and stir on medium-low heat until Velveeta is melted.

2. Spoon ¼ cup meat mixture in center of each tortilla; roll up. Place tortillas, seam-side down, in microwavable baking dish. Top with remaining ½ cup salsa and Velveeta. Cover loosely with microwavable plastic wrap.

3. Microwave on HIGH 4 to 6 minutes or until Velveeta is melted.

Makes 5 servings

Szechuan Pork & Vegetables

4 butterflied pork loin chops, ½ inch thick (1 to 1¼ pounds)
¼ cup plus 1 tablespoon stir-fry sauce, divided
¾ teaspoon bottled minced ginger *or* ½ teaspoon ground ginger
1 package (16 ounces) frozen Asian-style vegetables, thawed
1 can (5 ounces) crisp chow mein noodles
2 tablespoons chopped green onion

1. Heat large, deep nonstick skillet over medium heat until hot; add pork. Spoon 1 tablespoon stir-fry sauce over pork; sprinkle with ginger. Cook 3 minutes. Turn pork; cook 3 minutes. Transfer pork to plate; set aside. Add vegetables and remaining ¼ cup stir-fry sauce to skillet. Cook over medium-low heat 3 minutes; add pork. Cook 3 minutes or until pork is no longer pink in center, stirring vegetables and turning pork once.

2. Arrange chow mein noodles around edges of 4 plates. Transfer pork to plates. Top noodles with vegetable mixture. Sprinkle with onion.   *Makes 4 servings*

Creamy Beef and Vegetable Casserole

Prep Time: *5 minutes*   **Cook Time:** *10 to 15 minutes*

1 pound lean ground beef
1 small onion, chopped
1 bag (16 ounces) BIRDS EYE® frozen Farm Fresh Mixtures Broccoli, Corn & Red Peppers
1 can (10¾ ounces) cream of mushroom soup

• In medium skillet, brown beef and onion; drain excess fat.

• Meanwhile, in large saucepan, cook vegetables according to package directions; drain.

• Stir in beef mixture and soup. Cook over medium heat until heated through.
Makes 4 servings

Right:
*Szechuan Pork &
Vegetables*

Rice and Chicken Wraps

8 boneless, skinless chicken tenderloins
2 cups water
1 box UNCLE BEN'S® Fast Cooking Recipe Long Grain & Wild Rice
½ cup ranch salad dressing
1 cup shredded lettuce
8 (10-inch) flour tortillas

1. Spray large skillet with nonstick cooking spray. Add chicken, cook over medium-high heat 10 to 12 minutes or until lightly browned on both sides. Add water, rice and contents of seasoning packet. Bring to a boil. Cover; reduce heat and simmer 10 minutes or until chicken is no longer pink in center and liquid is absorbed. Stir in salad dressing.

2. Spoon rice mixture evenly down center of each tortilla; top with lettuce. Fold in both sides of tortillas; roll up tortilla tightly from bottom, keeping filling firmly packed. Slice each wrap diagonally into 2 pieces.   *Makes 4 servings*

Easy Chicken & Stuffing Skillet

4 tablespoons butter or margarine, divided
4 small boneless skinless chicken breast halves (about 1 pound)
1 package (6 ounces) STOVE TOP® Stuffing Mix for Chicken
2 cups frozen mixed vegetables
1⅔ cups water

MELT 2 tablespoons of the butter in large nonstick skillet on medium-high heat. Add chicken; cover. Cook 4 minutes on each side or until cooked through. Remove from skillet.

ADD contents of Vegetable/Seasoning packet, vegetables, water and remaining 2 tablespoons butter; bring to boil. Reduce heat to low; cover and simmer 5 minutes. Stir in Stuffing Crumbs just to moisten. Top with chicken; cover. Cook on low heat 5 minutes.   *Makes 4 servings*

Quick Tip

To warm tortillas, stack 8 to 12 and wrap them in plastic wrap. Microwave at HIGH about 40 to 50 seconds, turning over and rotating 1/4 turn once during heating. For 1 or 2 tortillas, wrap and heat at HIGH about 20 seconds.

Right:
Rice and Chicken Wraps

Tuna & Noodles

Prep Time: 10 *minutes*　　**Cook Time:** 15 *minutes*

2¼ **cups water**
3 **cups (6 ounces) medium egg noodles, uncooked**
¾ **pound (12 ounces) VELVEETA® Pasteurized Prepared Cheese Product, cut up**
1 **package (16 ounces) frozen vegetable blend, thawed, drained**
1 **can (6 ounces) tuna, drained, flaked**
¼ **teaspoon black pepper**

1. Bring water to boil in saucepan. Stir in noodles. Reduce heat to medium-low; cover. Simmer 8 minutes or until noodles are tender.

2. Add Velveeta, vegetables, tuna and pepper; stir until Velveeta is melted.

Makes 4 to 6 servings

Grilled Corn Soup

4 **ears Grilled Corn-on-the-Cob (recipe follows)**
5 **green onions**
4 **cups chicken broth, divided**
　Salt and black pepper

Cut kernels from cobs to make 2 to 2½ cups. Slice green onions, separating the white slices from the green. Place corn, white part of onions and 2 cups chicken broth in blender or food processor; process until mixture is slightly lumpy. Place corn mixture in large saucepan; add remaining chicken broth. Simmer gently 15 minutes. Stir in sliced green onion tops; season to taste with salt and pepper.

Makes 4 to 6 servings

Grilled Corn-on-the-Cob: Turn back corn husks; do not remove. Remove silks with stiff brush; rinse corn under cold running water. Smooth husks back into position. Grill ears, on a covered grill, over medium-hot KINGSFORD® briquets, about 25 minutes or until tender, turning corn often. Remove husks and serve.

Right:
Tuna & Noodles

Vegetarian Stir-Fry

Prep Time: *2 minutes*   **Cook Time:** *12 to 15 minutes*

1 bag (16 ounces) BIRDS EYE® frozen Mixed Vegetables
2 tablespoons water
1 can (14 ounces) kidney beans, drained
1 jar (14 ounces) spaghetti sauce
½ teaspoon garlic powder
½ cup grated Parmesan cheese

• In large skillet, place vegetables in water. Cover; cook 7 to 10 minutes over medium heat.

• Uncover; add beans, spaghetti sauce and garlic powder; cook until hot. Sprinkle with cheese. Serve over hot cooked rice or pasta.   *Makes 4 servings*

Campbell's® Easy Beef & Pasta

Prep and Cook Time: *20 minutes*

1 pound boneless beef sirloin steak, ¾ inch thick
1 tablespoon vegetable oil
1 can (10¾ ounces) CAMPBELL'S® Condensed Tomato Soup
½ cup water
1 bag (about 16 ounces) frozen side dish seasoned pasta and vegetable combination

1. Slice beef into very thin strips.

2. In medium skillet over medium-high heat, heat oil. Add beef and cook until beef is browned and juices evaporate, stirring often.

3. Add soup, water and vegetable combination. Heat to a boil. Reduce heat to low. Cover and cook 5 minutes or until beef and vegetables are done, stirring occasionally.   *Makes 4 servings*

Smart Tip

For easier slicing of beef, place it in the freezer for 45 to 60 minutes until it is partially frozen. Then, cut it into very thin slices.

Right:
Vegetarian Stir-Fry

Marinades & Sauces

Right:
Mustard
Vinaigrette (recipe
on page 182)

Complement a good piece of poultry, meat or fish with a flavorful marinade or sauce that adds the final touch and brings out its full flavor. Simple fruits and other desserts become temptations beyond compare when embellished with a splendid sweet sauce.

Ham Glaze
Prep Time: *10 minutes*

1 cup KARO® Light or Dark Corn Syrup
½ cup packed brown sugar
3 tablespoons prepared mustard
½ teaspoon ground ginger
   Dash ground cloves

1. In medium saucepan, combine corn syrup, brown sugar, mustard, ginger and cloves. Bring to boil over medium heat; boil 5 minutes, stirring constantly.

2. Brush on ham frequently during last 30 minutes of baking.   *Makes about 1 cup*

Microwave Directions: In 1½-quart microwavable bowl, combine all ingredients. Microwave on HIGH 6 minutes. Glaze ham as above.

Zippy Tartar Sauce for Grilled Fish
Prep Time: *5 minutes*

1 cup mayonnaise
3 tablespoons *Frank's*® *RedHot*® Sauce
2 tablespoons *French's*® Hearty Deli Brown Mustard
2 tablespoons sweet pickle relish
1 tablespoon minced capers

Combine mayonnaise, **RedHot** Sauce, mustard, pickle relish and capers in medium bowl. Cover and chill in refrigerator until ready to serve. Serve with grilled salmon, halibut, swordfish or tuna.   *Makes 1½ cups sauce*

Right:
Ham Glaze

Sweet 'n' Smoky BBQ Sauce

Prep Time: *5 minutes*

½ **cup ketchup**
⅓ **cup** *French's®* **Hearty Deli Brown Mustard**
⅓ **cup light molasses**
¼ **cup** *French's®* **Worcestershire Sauce**
¼ **teaspoon liquid smoke or hickory salt (optional)**

Combine ketchup, mustard, molasses, Worcestershire and liquid smoke, if desired, in medium bowl. Mix until well blended. Brush on chicken or ribs during last 15 minutes of grilling.

Makes about 1½ cups sauce

Dijon Vinaigrette

½ **fresh lemon**
3 **tablespoons honey-Dijon mustard**
2 **tablespoons red wine vinegar**
1 **clove garlic, minced**
½ **teaspoon Worcestershire sauce**
⅓ **cup extra-virgin olive oil**

1. To juice lemon, remove any visible seeds with tip of utility knife. Using citrus reamer or, squeezing tightly with hand, squeeze juice from lemon into small bowl. Remove any remaining seeds from bowl; discard.

2. Add mustard, vinegar, garlic and Worcestershire; whisk to blend. Gradually whisk in oil.

Makes ⅔ cup

Quick Tip

No time for last-minute salad preparation? It's easy to make a tossed salad ahead. Simply place vegetables, meat or poultry in the bottom of a salad bowl and add the dressing. Place salad greens on top; don't toss. Refrigerate for up to 2 hours. Toss the salad just before serving.

Right:
Sweet 'n' Smoky BBQ Sauce

Mushroom Bacon Sauce

5 slices bacon, cut into ¼-inch pieces (about 4 ounces)
1 (10-ounce) package mushrooms, sliced (about 4 cups)
¼ cup A.1.® Steak Sauce
2 tablespoons sherry cooking wine

Cook bacon in large skillet over medium-high heat until crisp. Remove bacon with slotted spoon. Reserve 2 tablespoons drippings.

Sauté mushrooms in same skillet in reserved drippings for 5 minutes or until tender. Stir in steak sauce, sherry and bacon; bring to a boil. Reduce heat; simmer 5 minutes. Serve hot with cooked beef, burgers or poultry.

Makes 1½ cups

Mustard Vinaigrette

2 tablespoons country-style Dijon mustard
½ cup seasoned rice vinegar
¼ cup vegetable oil
½ teaspoon dark sesame oil
Dash black pepper

Whisk together all ingredients in small bowl.

Makes about ¾ cup

Chili Marinade

¼ cup A.1.® Steak Sauce
¼ cup chili sauce

In small nonmetal bowl, combine steak sauce and chili sauce. Use to marinate beef or pork for about 1 hour in the refrigerator.

Makes ½ cup

Smart Tip

Sesame oil is a strong-tasting oil made from sesame seeds. It is used in small amounts for flavoring Oriental foods as well as dressings and sauces. Do not substitute it for other oils, such as olive oil.

Right:
Mushroom Bacon Sauce

Basil Mayonnaise

½ cup mayonnaise
½ cup sour cream or plain yogurt
1 green onion, cut into 1-inch pieces
2 tablespoons fresh parsley
2 tablespoons fresh basil
Salt and pepper

Combine mayonnaise, sour cream, onion, parsley and basil in food processor or blender; process until well blended. Season with salt and pepper to taste. Serve with poached or grilled salmon.

Makes about 1 cup

Lemon Pepper Marinade

⅔ cup A.1.® Steak Sauce
4 teaspoons grated lemon peel
1½ teaspoons coarsely ground black pepper

In small nonmetal bowl, combine steak sauce, lemon peel and pepper. Use to marinate beef, fish, poultry or pork for about 1 hour in the refrigerator.

Makes about ⅔ cup

Easy Tartar Sauce

¼ cup fat-free or reduced-fat mayonnaise
2 tablespoons sweet pickle relish
1 teaspoon lemon juice

Combine mayonnaise, relish and lemon juice in small bowl; mix well. Refrigerate until ready to serve.

Makes about ¼ cup

Right:
Basil Mayonnaise

Below:
Italian Marinade

Italian Marinade

**1 envelope GOOD SEASONS® Italian, Zesty Italian or Garlic & Herb
   Salad Dressing Mix**
⅓ cup oil
⅓ cup dry white wine or water
2 tablespoons lemon juice

Mix salad dressing mix, oil, wine and lemon juice in cruet or medium bowl until well blended. Reserve ¼ cup marinade for basting; refrigerate. Pour remaining marinade over 1½ to 2 pounds meat, poultry or seafood. Toss to coat well; cover. Refrigerate to marinate. Drain before grilling.   *Makes ⅔ cup*

Salsa Cruda

1 cup chopped tomato
2 tablespoons minced onion
2 tablespoons minced fresh cilantro (optional)
2 tablespoons lime juice
½ jalapeño pepper,* seeded, minced
1 clove garlic, minced

*Jalapeño peppers can sting and irritate the skin; wear rubber gloves when handling peppers and do not touch eyes. Wash hands after handling peppers.

Combine tomato, onion, cilantro, lime juice, jalapeño and garlic in small bowl. Stir to combine. Serve over hot quesadillas.   *Makes 4 servings*

Fajita Marinade

½ cup lime juice *or* ¼ cup lime juice and ¼ cup tequilla or beer
1 tablespoon dried oregano leaves
1 tablespoon minced garlic
2 teaspoons ground cumin
2 teaspoons black pepper

Combine all ingredients in small bowl; mix well. Use to marinate fajita meat or chicken for 1 hour in refrigerator. *Makes about ½ cup*

Sour Cream Sauce

¾ cup sour cream
2 tablespoons prepared horseradish
1 tablespoon balsamic vinegar
½ teaspoon sugar

Combine all ingredients in small bowl; mix well. *Makes about 1 cup*

Note: Sour Cream Sauce may be stored, covered, in refrigerator up to 1 day.

Buttermilk-Herb Dressing

½ cup plus 1 tablespoon low-fat buttermilk
3 tablespoons raspberry-flavored vinegar
1 tablespoon chopped fresh basil leaves
1½ teaspoons snipped fresh chives
¼ teaspoon minced garlic

Place all ingredients in small bowl; stir to combine. *Makes about ¾ cup*

Note: Buttermilk-Herb Dressing may be stored, covered, in refrigerator up to 1 day.

Above:
Buttermilk-Herb Dressing

Smart Tip

Try chewing a piece of bread while peeling and chopping onions, as it might help to minimize the tears. When onions are cut, they release sulfur compounds that irritate the eyes.

Onion Wine Sauce

4 cups onion wedges
2 cloves garlic, minced
2 tablespoons margarine or butter
½ cup A.1.® Original or A.1.® BOLD & SPICY Steak Sauce
2 tablespoons red cooking wine

In large skillet, over medium-high heat, cook and stir onions and garlic in margarine until tender, about 10 minutes. Stir in steak sauce and wine; heat to a boil. Reduce heat; simmer 5 minutes. Serve hot with cooked steak.

Makes 2 ½ cups

Pineapple Salsa

½ cup finely chopped fresh pineapple
¼ cup finely chopped red bell pepper
1 green onion, thinly sliced
2 tablespoons lime juice
½ jalapeño pepper,* seeded, minced
1 tablespoon chopped fresh cilantro or fresh basil

*Jalapeño peppers can sting and irritate the skin; wear rubber gloves when handling peppers and do not touch eyes. Wash hands after handling peppers.

Combine all ingredients in small nonmetallic bowl. Serve at room temperature.

Makes 4 servings

Right:
Onion Wine Sauce

Fresh Fruit Sauce

½ cup KARO® Light Corn Syrup
2 cups fresh berries, chopped kiwifruit or chopped peaches
1 teaspoon lemon juice
¼ teaspoon almond extract *or* ½ cup chopped fresh fruit

1. In blender or food processor combine corn syrup, 2 cups fruit and lemon juice. Process until smooth.

2. Stir in your choice of almond extract or chopped fresh fruit.

Makes about 2 cups

Hot Fudge

Prep Time: 5 *minutes*   **Cook Time:** 15 *minutes*

1 cup FLEISCHMANN'S® Original Margarine
1 cup skim milk
5 ounces unsweetened chocolate
⅔ cup corn syrup
⅔ cup sugar
Salt to taste

1. Heat margarine, milk and chocolate in top of double boiler over barely simmering water, stirring constantly until chocolate and margarine are melted and smooth.

2. Add corn syrup, sugar and salt, stirring constantly until the sugar dissolves and the mixture is smooth.

3. Cover and store in refrigerator. Serve warm.

Makes about 3½ cups

Right:
Fresh Fruit Sauce

Strawberry Sauce

1 pint strawberries, hulled
2 to 3 tablespoons sugar
1 tablespoon strawberry- or orange-flavored liqueur (optional)

Combine strawberries, sugar and liqueur, if desired, in blender or food processor. Cover; process until smooth. Serve over waffles or pancakes.   *Makes 1½ cups*

Maple Walnut Raisin Sauce
Prep Time: 10 minutes

1 cup KARO® Light or Dark Corn Syrup
½ cup packed brown sugar
½ cup heavy or whipping cream
½ cup coarsely chopped walnuts
¼ cup raisins
½ teaspoon maple-flavored extract

1. In medium saucepan combine corn syrup, brown sugar and cream. Stirring constantly, bring to full boil over medium heat and boil 1 minute. Remove from heat.

2. Stir in walnuts, raisins and maple extract. Serve warm. Store in refrigerator.

Makes 2 cups

Smart Tip

After opening, wrap raisins securely in plastic wrap or store in an airtight container at room temperature. They will keep for several months. If refrigerated in a tightly covered container, raisins will keep for up to one year.

Right:
Strawberry Sauce

Honey Berry Purée

2 cups blackberries or raspberries
¼ cup honey
2 tablespoons fruit-flavored or regular brandy (optional)

Purée blackberries in blender or food processor. If desired, press through sieve to remove seeds. Or, mash berries with fork. Stir in honey and brandy, if desired, until blended. Serve over angel food cake or sliced fruit.　　　*Makes 2 cups*

Favorite recipe from **National Honey Board**

Gingered Peach Sauce

1 can (16 ounces) sliced peaches in unsweetened juice, drained
1½ teaspoons minced fresh ginger
2 tablespoons almond-flavored liqueur (optional)

Place peaches in food processor container fitted with steel blade; cover and process until smooth, scraping down sides of container once. Add ginger and liqueur, if desired; process until smooth. Serve with fresh fruit.

Makes about 1 cup

Heavenly Kahlúa® Fudge Sauce

1 (16-ounce) can chocolate fudge topping
¼ cup KAHLÚA® Liqueur

In saucepan (or microwavable bowl), heat fudge topping (or microwave at HIGH) until melted; stir in Kahlúa®. Serve warm. To store, cover and refrigerate; reheat as needed.　　　*Makes 1⅔ cups*

Right:
Gingered Peach Sauce

Hot Chocolate Fudge Sauce

Prep Time: 10 *minutes, plus cooling*

¾ **cup sugar**
¾ **cup heavy or whipping cream**
½ **cup KARO® Light Corn Syrup**
  2 **tablespoons margarine or butter**
  1 **package (8 ounces) semisweet chocolate**
  1 **teaspoon vanilla**

1. In large saucepan combine sugar, cream, corn syrup and margarine. Stirring constantly, bring to full boil over medium heat. Remove from heat.

2. Stir in chocolate until melted. Stir in vanilla.

3. Serve warm over ice cream. Store in refrigerator.   *Makes about 2¼ cups*

Ever-So-Good Peanut Butter Sauce

Prep Time: 5 *minutes*

½ **cup KARO® Light or Dark Corn Syrup**
½ **cup SKIPPY® SUPER CHUNK® or Creamy Peanut Butter**
  3 **to 4 tablespoons milk**

1. In small bowl stir corn syrup, peanut butter and milk until blended.

2. Serve over ice cream or cake. Store in refrigerator.   *Makes about 1¼ cups*

Right (top to bottom):
Hot Chocolate Fudge Sauce, Ever-So-Good Peanut Butter Sauce and Maple Walnut Raisin Sauce (page 192)

Creamy Lime Dipping Sauce

1 container (6 ounces) nonfat vanilla yogurt
2 tablespoons minced fresh cilantro
2 tablespoons lime juice
1 tablespoon minced jalapeño pepper*

*Jalapeño peppers can sting and irritate the skin; wear rubber gloves when handling peppers and do not touch eyes. Wash hands after handling peppers.

Combine all ingredients in small bowl; mix well to combine. Serve with sliced fresh fruit.   *Makes about 1 cup*

Espresso Sauce
Prep Time: *10 minutes*

1 cup water
½ cup ground espresso coffee beans
1 (14-ounce) can EAGLE® BRAND Sweetened Condensed Milk (NOT evaporated milk)
¼ cup (½ stick) butter or margarine

In small saucepan over medium heat, bring 1 cup water and ground espresso to a boil. Remove from heat and let stand 5 minutes. Pour mixture through fine wire-mesh strainer; discard grounds. In small saucepan over medium heat, combine espresso and **Eagle Brand.** Bring to a boil. Remove from heat; stir in butter. Cool.
Makes 1¼ cups

Right:
Creamy Lime
Dipping Sauce

Banana Praline Sauce

Prep Time: 15 *minutes*   **Cook Time:** 5 *minutes*

¼ **cup margarine**
¼ **cup packed brown sugar**
 2 **teaspoons lemon juice**
½ **teaspoon ground cinnamon**
 1 **cup sliced banana**
¼ **cup PLANTERS® Walnuts, chopped**

1. Heat margarine, brown sugar, lemon juice and cinnamon in saucepan over medium heat until margarine melts and mixture is smooth.

2. Stir in banana. Cook for 2 to 3 minutes or until fruit is tender. Stir in walnuts. Cool. Cover and store in refrigerator.

3. Serve sauce warm over ice cream or frozen yogurt.   *Makes 1½ cups*

Peach Melba Sauce

Prep Time: 10 *minutes*   **Cook Time:** 5 *minutes*

 1 **(10-ounce) package frozen raspberries in syrup, thawed**
¼ **cup FLEISCHMANN'S® Original Margarine**
 1 **teaspoon ground cinnamon**
¼ **teaspoon ground nutmeg**
 1 **(15-ounce) can peach slices in light syrup, drained**

1. Heat raspberries with syrup, margarine, cinnamon and nutmeg in saucepan over medium-high heat to a boil.

2. Reduce heat; simmer for 3 to 5 minutes or until slightly thickened. Stir in peaches. Cool. Cover and store in refrigerator.

3. Serve fruit sauce warm or cold over ice cream or frozen yogurt.   *Makes 2 cups*

Right:
Hot Fudge (page 190), Banana Praline Sauce and Peach Melba Sauce

Salads & Sides

Once you've created a tantalizing meal in minutes, why not enhance it with a healthful salad or an attractive side dish? When teamed-up with these sure-fire dishes, the centerpiece of your meal will reach heavenly heights . . . with minimal effort.

Right:
*Grilled Chicken
Caesar Salad
(recipe on
page 212)*

Smart Tip

Cherry tomatoes, with their small, bite-size round shapes, are often used as a garnish or salad ingredient. Wash tomatoes just before using and remove any stems that are present. Choose tomatoes that are firm.

Right:
Green Bean and Potato Salad

Green Bean and Potato Salad

Dijon Vinaigrette (optional, page 180, or prepared vinaigrette dressing)
1½ pounds small red-skin potatoes
10 ounces fresh green beans
1 cup quartered cherry tomatoes
½ cup chopped onion
⅛ teaspoon salt
⅛ teaspoon black pepper

1. Prepare Dijon Vinaigrette, if desired; set aside.

2. Scrub potatoes under cold running water with soft vegetable brush; rinse well. Do not peel.

3. Place potatoes in 3-quart saucepan; cover with water. Bring to a boil over medium-high heat. Reduce heat to low; simmer, covered, 10 to 15 minutes until fork-tender.

4. Drain potatoes in colander. Rinse under cold running water; drain. Cut potatoes lengthwise into halves with large utility knife; set aside.

5. Rinse beans thoroughly in colander under cold running water; drain. Snap off stem end from each bean; discard. Cut beans into 2-inch pieces with utility knife.

6. Place beans in 2-quart saucepan; cover with water. Bring to a boil over medium-high heat. Reduce heat to low; simmer, covered, 5 to 6 minutes until beans are crisp-tender.

7. Transfer beans to colander; rinse under cold running water. Drain; set aside.

8. Combine potatoes, beans, tomatoes and onion in large bowl. Add Dijon Vinaigrette, if desired, and salt and pepper; toss well. Cover tightly with plastic wrap. Refrigerate 2 to 3 hours.   *Makes 6 servings*

Cabbage Salad

4 cups shredded cabbage (about ½ head)
2 tablespoons FILIPPO BERIO® Olive Oil
2 tablespoons lemon juice
   Salt and freshly ground black pepper
   Onion rings and green bell pepper rings (optional)

In large bowl, place cabbage. In small bowl, whisk together olive oil and lemon juice. Pour over cabbage; toss until lightly coated. Season to taste with salt and black pepper. Garnish with onion and bell pepper rings, if desired.

Makes 4 to 6 servings

Apple-Rice Medley

1 package (6 ounces) long-grain and wild rice mix
1 cup (4 ounces) shredded mild Cheddar cheese, divided
1 cup chopped Washington Golden Delicious apple
1 cup sliced mushrooms
½ cup thinly sliced celery

Prepare rice mix according to package directions. Preheat oven to 350°F. Add ½ cup cheese, apple, mushrooms and celery to rice; toss to combine. Spoon mixture into 1-quart casserole dish. Bake 15 minutes. Top with remaining ½ cup cheese; bake until cheese melts, about 10 minutes. *Makes 4 servings*

Microwave Directions: Combine cooked rice, ½ cup cheese, apple, mushrooms and celery as directed; spoon mixture into 1-quart microwave-safe dish. Microwave at HIGH 3 to 4 minutes or until heated through. Top with remaining ½ cup cheese; microwave at HIGH 1 minute or until cheese melts.

Favorite recipe from **Washington Apple Commission**

Serving Tip

Serve salads with warm crusty French bread wrapped in a napkin to retain warmth. Brush bread with garlic butter before warming for extra flavor.

Right:
Apple-Rice Medley

Spinach-Tomato Salad

Prep Time: *10 minutes*

  1 **package (8 ounces) DOLE® Complete Spinach Salad**
  2 **medium tomatoes, halved and cut into thin wedges**
 ½ **medium cucumber, thinly sliced**
 ½ **small onion, thinly sliced**
  1 **can (14 to 16 ounces) low-sodium kidney or garbanzo beans, drained**

• Toss spinach, croutons and bacon from salad bag with tomatoes, cucumber, onion and beans in medium serving bowl.

• Pour dressing from packet over salad; toss to coat evenly.   *Makes 4 servings*

Right:
Spinach-Tomato Salad

Roasted Potato and Vegetable Salad

Prep Time: *10 minutes*   **Bake Time:** *45 minutes*

  2 **pounds red potatoes, cubed**
  2 **zucchini, thinly sliced lengthwise**
  2 **carrots, diagonally sliced**
  1 **small red onion, cut into wedges**
  2 **cups KRAFT® TASTE OF LIFE™ Tomato & Garlic Dressing**

TOSS vegetables with dressing in large bowl.

SPOON into shallow roasting pan.

BAKE at 400°F for 40 to 45 minutes or until vegetables are tender, stirring occasionally.   *Makes 8 servings*

Above:
Roasted Potato and Vegetable Salad

Beef & Blue Cheese Salad

Prep Time: 10 *minutes*

1 package (10 ounces) mixed green lettuce leaves
4 ounces sliced rare deli roast beef, cut into thin strips
1 large tomato, seeded and coarsely chopped *or* 8 large cherry tomatoes, halved
2 ounces (½ cup) crumbed Gorgonzola or blue cheese
1 cup croutons
½ cup prepared Caesar or Italian salad dressing

1. In large bowl, combine lettuce, roast beef, tomato, cheese and croutons.

2. Drizzle with dressing; toss well. Serve immediately.

Makes 4 main-dish or 8 side-dish servings

Serving Suggestion: Serve with warm crusty breadsticks.

Cole Slaw Vinaigrette

¼ cup vegetable oil
2 tablespoons white wine vinegar
1 tablespoon honey
Salt and pepper
1 (8-ounce) package cole slaw mix

Whisk together oil, vinegar and honey. Season with salt and pepper to taste. Place cole slaw mix in medium bowl; pour vinaigrette over mix. Toss lightly to coat; cover. Refrigerate for 30 minutes or up to 3 days.   *Makes 4 servings*

Smart Tip

Gorgonzola, one of Italy's great cheeses, is made from cow's milk and has a creamy, savory flavor. It can be found cut into wedges and wrapped in foil in most supermarkets.

Right:
Beef & Blue Cheese Salad

Spinach-Orange Salad

1 large bunch spinach, stems removed
2 oranges
½ small jicama, peeled and cut into julienne strips (about 1 cup)
¼ cup toasted pecan halves
  Prepared vinaigrette dressing (optional)

Wash and dry spinach; chill until very crisp. Tear into bite-size pieces; place in large bowl. Peel oranges, removing white membrane. Cut between orange segments and membranes; discard membranes. Chop orange segments. Add oranges, jicama and pecans to spinach. Pour vinaigrette over spinach mixture, if desired, and toss gently until well mixed.   *Makes 6 servings*

Grilled Chicken Caesar Salad

Prep Time: 15 *minutes plus marinating*   **Grill Time:** 20 *minutes*

8 cups torn romaine lettuce
1 pound boneless skinless chicken breasts, grilled, cut into strips
1 cup seasoned croutons
½ cup KRAFT® Shredded or 100% Grated Parmesan Cheese
¾ cup KRAFT FREE® Caesar Italian Fat Free Dressing

TOSS lettuce, chicken, croutons and cheese in large salad bowl.

ADD dressing; toss to coat. Serve with fresh lemon wedges and fresh ground pepper, if desired.   *Makes 4 servings*

Variation: Prepare as directed, substituting 1 package (10 ounces) mixed or romaine salad greens.

Right:
Spinach-Orange
Salad

Carpaccio di Zucchini

Prep and Cook Time: *28 minutes*

¾ **pound zucchini, shredded**
½ **cup sliced almonds, toasted**
1 **tablespoon prepared Italian dressing**
4 **French bread baguettes, sliced in half lengthwise**
4 **teaspoons soft spread margarine**
3 **tablespoons grated Parmesan cheese**

1. Preheat broiler. Place zucchini in medium bowl. Add almonds and dressing; mix well. Set aside.

2. Place baguette halves on large baking sheet; spread evenly with margarine. Sprinkle with cheese. Broil 3 inches from heat 2 to 3 minutes or until edges and cheese are browned.

3. Spread zucchini mixture evenly on each baguette half. Garnish as desired. Serve immediately. *Makes 4 servings*

Go-with suggestions: Spaghetti with tomato sauce.

Right:
Carpaccio di Zucchini

Vegetable-Stuffed Baked Potatoes

1 jar (16 ounces) RAGÚ® Cheese Creations!® Roasted Garlic Parmesan Sauce or Double Cheddar Sauce
1 bag (16 ounces) frozen assorted vegetables, cooked and drained
6 large baking potatoes, unpeeled and baked

In 2-quart saucepan, heat Ragú Cheese Creations! Sauce. Stir in vegetables; heat through.

Cut a lengthwise slice from top of each potato. Lightly mash pulp in each potato. Evenly spoon sauce mixture onto each potato. Sprinkle, if desired, with ground black pepper.

Makes 6 servings

Campbell's® Creamy Vegetable Medley

Prep Time: *15 minutes*   **Cook Time:** *20 minutes*

1 can (10¾ ounces) CAMPBELL'S® Condensed Cream of Celery Soup *or* 98% Fat Free Cream of Celery Soup
½ cup milk
2 cups broccoli flowerets
2 medium carrots, sliced (about 1 cup)
1 cup cauliflower flowerets

1. In medium saucepan mix soup, milk, broccoli, carrots and cauliflower. Over medium heat, heat to a boil.

2. Reduce heat to low. Cover and cook 15 minutes or until vegetables are tender, stirring occasionally.

Makes 6 servings

Variation: Omit milk. Substitute 1 bag (16 ounces) frozen vegetable combination (broccoli, cauliflower, carrots) for fresh vegetables.

Right:
Vegetable-Stuffed Baked Potato

Broccoli and Onion Casserole

    1 large onion
    ¾ cup defatted low sodium chicken broth*
  1 ¼ pounds broccoli
    ½ teaspoon black pepper, divided
      Dash paprika

*To defat chicken broth, skim fat from surface of broth with spoon. Or, place can of broth in refrigerator at least 2 hours ahead of time. Before using, remove fat that has hardened on surface of broth.

Preheat oven to 375°F. Cut onion into quarters, then crosswise into thin slices. Bring onion and chicken broth to a boil, in medium saucepan, over high heat. Reduce heat to low. Simmer, covered, 5 minutes or until onion is fork-tender. Remove onion to small bowl with slotted spoon, leaving broth in saucepan. Set aside.

Trim broccoli, removing tough part of stems. Cut into florets with ½-inch stems. Peel remaining broccoli stems; cut into ¼-inch-thick slices. Spread half of broccoli in 8-inch square baking dish or 2-quart casserole. Spread half of onion slices on broccoli. Sprinkle with ¼ teaspoon pepper. Repeat layers.

Pour reserved broth over vegetables. Cover tightly with foil. Bake 25 minutes or until broccoli is tender. *Do not stir.* Drain liquid; sprinkle with paprika before serving.

Makes 6 servings

Pepperidge Farm® Sausage Corn Bread Stuffing

Prep Time: 15 *minutes*   **Cook Time:** 25 *minutes*

- ¼ **pound bulk pork sausage**
- 1 ¼ **cups water**
- ½ **cup cooked whole kernel corn**
- ½ **cup shredded Cheddar cheese (2 ounces)**
- 1 **tablespoon chopped fresh parsley** *or* 1 **teaspoon dried parsley flakes**
- 4 **cups PEPPERIDGE FARM® Corn Bread Stuffing**

1. In large saucepan over medium-high heat, cook sausage until browned, stirring to separate meat. Pour off fat.

2. Stir in water, corn, cheese and parsley. Add stuffing. Mix lightly. Spoon into greased 1 ½-quart casserole.

3. Cover and bake at 350°F. for 25 minutes or until hot.   *Makes 6 servings*

Tip: This stuffing bake brings a new flavor to the traditional holiday meal—and is easy enough for an everyday meal!

Calico Corn

Prep Time: 2 *to* 3 *minutes*   **Cook Time:** 6 *to* 8 *minutes*

- 1 **bag (16 ounces) BIRDS EYE® frozen Corn**
- ½ **cup finely diced green pepper**
- ½ **cup chopped tomato**

- Cook corn according to package directions.

- Combine corn with green pepper and tomato.

- Add salt and pepper to taste.   *Makes 4 to 6 servings*

Smart Tip

In season, tomatoes should be plump and heavy with a vibrant color and a pleasant aroma. They should be firm but not hard. A soft tomato will either be watery or overripe. Avoid those that are cracked or have soft spots.

Smart Tip

For faster, more even cooking of Brussels sprouts, cut an "X" deep into the stem end of each sprout.

Right:
Holiday Vegetable Bake

Above:
Broth-Braised Brussels Sprouts

Holiday Vegetable Bake
Prep Time: *5 minutes*   **Cook Time:** *10 minutes*

1 package (16 ounces) frozen vegetable combination
1 can (10¾ ounces) condensed cream of broccoli soup
⅓ cup milk
1⅓ cups *French's*® *Taste Toppers*™ French Fried Onions, divided

Microwave Directions: Combine vegetables, soup, milk and ⅔ *cup* **Taste Toppers** in 2-quart microwavable casserole. Microwave,* uncovered, on HIGH 10 to 12 minutes or until vegetables are crisp-tender, stirring halfway through cooking time. Sprinkle with remaining ⅔ *cup* **Taste Toppers.** Microwave 1 minute or until **Taste Toppers** are golden.   *Makes 4 to 6 servings*

*Or, bake in preheated 375°F oven 30 to 35 minutes.

Broth-Braised Brussels Sprouts

1 pound fresh Brussels sprouts
½ cup condensed beef broth *or* ½ cup water plus 2 teaspoons instant
    beef bouillon granules
1 tablespoon butter or margarine, softened
¼ cup freshly grated Parmesan cheese
    Paprika

1. Trim stems from Brussels sprouts and pull off discolored outer leaves.

2. Use large enough saucepan to allow sprouts to fit in single layer. Place sprouts and broth in saucepan. Bring to a boil; reduce heat. Cover; simmer about 5 minutes or just until sprouts turn bright green and are crisp-tender.

3. Uncover; simmer until liquid is almost evaporated. Toss cooked sprouts with butter, then cheese. Sprinkle with paprika to taste. Garnish as desired.
                    Makes 4 side-dish servings

Easy Veggie-Topped Baked Spuds
Prep and Cook Time: *23 minutes*

2½ cups frozen broccoli-carrot vegetable medley
4 large baking potatoes
1 can (10¾ ounces) cream of broccoli soup
½ cup (2 ounces) shredded Cheddar cheese
Salt and pepper

1. Place vegetables in microwavable bowl. Microwave at HIGH 5 minutes; drain.

2. Scrub potatoes; pierce several times with knife. Microwave at HIGH 15 minutes or until potatoes are soft.

3. While potatoes are cooking, combine soup, vegetables and cheese in medium saucepan. Cook and stir over low heat until cheese melts and mixture is heated through.

4. Split baked potatoes in half. Top each potato with soup mixture. Season to taste with salt and pepper.   *Makes 4 servings*

Vegetable Stir-Fry

1 tablespoon vegetable oil
3 to 4 carrots, diagonally sliced
2 zucchini, diagonally sliced
3 tablespoons orange juice
Salt and pepper

Heat oil in medium skillet or wok over medium heat. Add carrots; stir-fry 3 minutes. Add zucchini and orange juice; stir-fry 4 minutes or until vegetables are crisp-tender. Season with salt and pepper to taste.   *Makes 4 servings*

Smart Tip

Choose russet or Idaho potatoes for baking. Store them in a cool, dark place for up to 2 weeks, away from onions (to prevent the potatoes from rotting more quickly).

Right:
Easy Veggie-Topped Baked Spuds

Grilled Corn-on-the-Cob

¼ **pound butter or margarine, softened**
1 **tablespoon KIKKOMAN® Soy Sauce**
½ **teaspoon dried tarragon leaves, crumbled**
6 **ears fresh corn**

Thoroughly blend butter, soy sauce and tarragon leaves. Husk corn. Lay each ear on piece of foil large enough to wrap around it; spread ears generously with seasoned butter. Wrap foil around corn; seal edges. Place on grill 3 inches from hot coals; cook 20 to 30 minutes, or until corn is tender, turning over frequently. (Or, place wrapped corn on baking sheet. Bake in 325°F oven 30 minutes.) Serve immediately.   *Makes 6 servings*

Note: Butter-soy mixture may also be spread on hot boiled corn.

Above:
*Grilled
Corn-on-the-Cob*

Lemon Basil Broccoli

Prep Time: *2 minutes*   **Cook Time:** *8 minutes*

1 **bag (16 ounces) BIRDS EYE® frozen Broccoli Cuts**
2 **tablespoons butter, melted**
¼ **teaspoon lemon juice**
¼ **teaspoon dried basil**

• Cook broccoli according to package directions; drain.

• Combine butter, lemon juice and basil in small bowl; mix well.

• Combine broccoli and butter mixture; toss to blend.   *Makes 4 servings*

Nutty Vegetable Duo

1 (10-ounce) package frozen green beans
½ (16-ounce) package frozen small whole onions
¼ cup toasted slivered almonds
2 tablespoons butter or margarine
   Salt and black pepper

1. Combine beans and onions in medium saucepan; cook according to package directions. Drain.

2. Return vegetables to saucepan. Add almonds and butter; stir over low heat until butter is melted and mixture is thoroughly heated. Season with salt and pepper to taste. *Makes 4 servings*

Note: To toast almonds, spread almonds evenly in shallow baking pan. Bake in 350°F oven 8 to 10 minutes or until lightly toasted, stirring occasionally.

Fresh Vegetable Sauté

2 tablespoons olive oil
6 cups assorted cut-up vegetables, such as broccoli flowerets, green
      beans, cauliflowerets, sugar snap peas, bell pepper strips, diagonally
      sliced carrots, mushrooms, onions, yellow squash and zucchini
1 envelope GOOD SEASONS® Italian Salad Dressing Mix
2 tablespoons red wine vinegar

HEAT oil in large skillet on medium-high heat. Add vegetables; cook and stir until crisp-tender.

ADD salad dressing mix and vinegar; cook and stir until heated through. Garnish with chopped fresh parsley, if desired. *Makes 4 to 6 servings*

Pace® Mexican-Style Mac 'n' Cheese
Prep Time: 5 *minutes*   **Cook Time:** 10 *minutes*

2 cups *uncooked* elbow macaroni
1 jar (15 ounces) PACE® Picante con Queso Dip

1. In large saucepan prepare macaroni according to package directions. Drain.

2. In same pan mix dip and macaroni. Over low heat, heat through, stirring occasionally.   *Makes 4 servings*

Pace® Queso Baked Potatoes
Prep Time: 10 *minutes*   **Cook Time:** 3 *minutes*

4 hot baked potatoes, split
1 cup PACE® Picante con Queso Dip

Microwave Directions:
1. Place hot baked potatoes on microwave-safe plate. Carefully fluff up potatoes with fork.

2. Spoon dip over potatoes. Microwave on HIGH 3 minutes or until hot.
Makes 4 servings

Note: To heat one potato: Top with ¼ cup dip. Microwave on HIGH 1 minute or until hot. Increase time to 2 minutes if using dip from the refrigerator.

Broccoli Queso Baked Potatoes: In step 2 top each potato with ¼ cup cooked broccoli cuts. Spoon dip over potatoes. Microwave on HIGH 3 minutes until hot.

Vegetable Queso Baked Potatoes: After microwaving potatoes with dip, top each potato with chopped tomato and sliced green onion.

Tip: To bake potatoes, pierce potatoes with fork. Bake at 400°F. for 1 hour or microwave on HIGH 10½ to 12½ minutes or until fork-tender.

Stuffed Tomatoes

    4 medium tomatoes
    ¼ cup grated Parmesan cheese
    4 eggs
    4 teaspoons minced green onion
    Salt and black pepper to taste
    Creamed Spinach (optional, recipe follows)

1. Preheat oven to 375°F.

2. Cut thin slice off blossom end of each tomato; remove seeds and pulp, being careful not to pierce side of tomato. Place tomato shells in shallow baking dish.

3. Sprinkle 1 tablespoon Parmesan cheese inside each tomato. Break an egg into each tomato. Top with onion, salt and pepper. Bake 15 to 20 minutes or until eggs are set. Serve with Creamed Spinach, if desired.   *Makes 4 servings*

Creamed Spinach

    1 package (10 ounces) frozen chopped spinach, thawed
    2 tablespoons butter or margarine
    2 tablespoons all-purpose flour
    1 cup milk
    ¼ teaspoon salt
    Dash black pepper
    1 tablespoon grated Parmesan cheese (optional)

1. Press spinach to remove all moisture; set aside. Melt butter in medium saucepan over medium heat. Stir in flour; cook until bubbly.

2. Slowly stir in milk. Cook until thickened. Add spinach; continue cooking over low heat, stirring constantly, about 5 minutes or until spinach is tender. Season with salt, pepper and cheese, if desired.   *Makes 4 servings*

Quick Tip

To save time and get the best results when pressing spinach, press it between two nested pie plates, tilting plates over sink to drain well.

Cheesy Rice & Broccoli

Prep Time: *5 minutes* **Cook Time:** *10 minutes plus standing*

1 package (10 ounces) frozen chopped broccoli, thawed, drained
1 cup water
1 ½ cups MINUTE® White Rice, uncooked
½ pound (8 ounces) VELVEETA® Pasteurized Prepared Cheese Product, cut up

1. Bring broccoli and water to full boil in medium saucepan on medium-high heat.

2. Stir in rice; cover. Remove from heat. Let stand 5 minutes.

3. Add Velveeta; stir until Velveeta is melted. *Makes 6 servings*

Mandarin Turkey Salad

Buttermilk-Herb Dressing (optional, recipe page 187)
1 can (about 14 ounces) fat-free reduced-sodium chicken broth
1 ¼ pounds turkey tenderloins, cut in half lengthwise
½ teaspoon dried basil leaves
½ pound (about 8 cups) mesclun salad greens, washed and dried
2 pounds (about 10 cups) raw cut-up salad bar vegetables such as broccoli florets, red or yellow bell peppers, carrots and red onion
1 can (11 ounces) mandarin orange segments, drained

Prepare Buttermilk-Herb Dressing, if desired. Set aside. Place broth in medium saucepan; bring to a boil over high heat. Add turkey and basil. Return to a boil; reduce heat. Simmer, covered, 12 to 14 minutes or until turkey is no longer pink. Remove turkey from broth. When cool enough to handle, shred turkey into strips. Arrange salad greens on individual plates. Divide turkey evenly over salad greens. Arrange vegetables and orange segments around turkey; drizzle each serving with 2 tablespoons Buttermilk-Herb Dressing, if desired. *Makes 6 servings*

Right:
Cheesy Rice &
Broccoli

Quick Tip

To reheat a frozen 1-quart casserole, unwrap and microwave, covered, at HIGH 10 to 15 minutes, stirring once or twice during cooking. Allow to stand about 5 minutes.

Right:
Cheesy Rice Casserole

Cheesy Rice Casserole
Prep Time: *15 minutes*   **Cook Time:** *9 minutes*

    2 cups hot cooked rice
1 ⅓ cups French's® Taste Toppers™ French Fried Onions, divided
    1 cup sour cream
    1 jar (16 ounces) medium salsa, divided
    1 cup (4 ounces) shredded Cheddar or taco blend cheese, divided

Combine rice and ⅔ cup **Taste Toppers** in large bowl. Spoon half of the rice mixture into microwavable 2-quart shallow casserole. Spread sour cream over rice mixture.

Layer half of the salsa and half of the cheese over sour cream. Sprinkle with remaining rice mixture, salsa and cheese. Cover loosely with plastic wrap. Microwave on HIGH 8 minutes or until heated through. Sprinkle with remaining ⅔ cup **Taste Toppers**. Microwave 1 minute or until **Taste Toppers** are golden.

Makes 6 servings

Pineapple Yam Casserole

    4 medium yams, cooked, peeled and mashed, *or* 2 (16- or 17-ounce) cans yams, drained and mashed
    ⅓ cup SMUCKER'S® Pineapple Topping
    4 tablespoons butter or margarine, melted, divided
    1 tablespoon lemon juice

Combine yams, pineapple topping, 3 tablespoons butter and lemon juice; mix well. Brush 1-quart casserole with remaining 1 tablespoon butter. Spoon yam mixture into casserole. Bake at 350°F for 25 minutes or until heated through.

Makes 4 servings

Steamed Broccoli & Carrots

    1 pound broccoli
   12 baby carrots, peeled*
    1 tablespoon butter or margarine
      Salt and black pepper

*Substitute ½ pound frozen baby carrots or ½ pound regular carrots, cut into 2-inch chunks, for baby carrots.

1. Break broccoli into flowerets. Discard large stems. Trim smaller stems; cut stems into thin slices.

2. Place 2 to 3 inches of water and steamer basket in large saucepan; bring water to a boil.

3. Add broccoli and carrots; cover. Steam 6 minutes or until vegetables are crisp-tender.

4. Place vegetables in serving bowl. Add butter; toss lightly to coat. Season with salt and pepper to taste.   *Makes 4 servings*

Salsa Macaroni & Cheese
Prep Time: 5 *minutes*   **Cook Time:** 15 *minutes*

    1 jar (16 ounces) RAGÚ® Cheese Creations!® Double Cheddar Sauce
    1 cup prepared mild salsa
    8 ounces elbow macaroni, cooked and drained

1. In 2-quart saucepan, heat Ragú Cheese Creations! Sauce over medium heat. Stir in salsa; heat through.

2. Toss with hot macaroni. Serve immediately.   *Makes 4 servings*

Swanson® Garlic Mashed Potatoes

Prep Time: 10 *minutes*   **Cook Time:** 15 *minutes*

2 cans (14½ ounces *each*) SWANSON® Seasoned Chicken Broth with Roasted Garlic
5 large potatoes, cut into 1-inch pieces

1. In medium saucepan place broth and potatoes. Over high heat, heat to a boil. Reduce heat to medium. Cover and cook 10 minutes or until potatoes are tender. Drain, reserving broth.

2. Mash potatoes with **1 ¼ *cups*** reserved broth. If needed, add additional broth until potatoes are desired consistency.   *Makes about 6 servings*

Skinny Mashed Potatoes: Substitute 2 cans (14½ ounces ***each***) SWANSON® Chicken Broth for Chicken Broth with Roasted Garlic.

Sweet-Sour Red Cabbage

   1 tablespoon butter or margarine
½ cup wine vinegar
¼ cup honey
   1 teaspoon salt
   1 medium head red cabbage, shredded (8 cups)
   2 apples, cored and diced

Melt butter in large nonstick skillet or stainless steel saucepan over medium heat. Stir in vinegar, honey and salt. Add cabbage and apples; toss well. Reduce heat to low; cover and simmer 45 to 50 minutes.   *Makes 4 to 6 servings*

Microwave Directions: Place shredded cabbage in 3-quart microwave-safe baking dish. Add apples, butter and vinegar. Cover and cook on HIGH (100%) 15 minutes. Stir in honey and salt. Cover and cook on HIGH 10 minutes.

Favorite recipe from **National Honey Board**

Quick Tip

If honey has crystallized, warm it in the microwave oven until it is pourable. Place the jar of honey, without the lid, in the microwave and heat at HIGH about 30 seconds. Stir the honey and let it stand 1 minute; repeat steps if necessary.

Brunch & Lunch
DISHES

Considered by many to be the day's most important meal, a good lunch or brunch can energize you for hours, but it shouldn't take hours to make. Our enticing yet easy recipes will get you out of the kitchen and doing all of the things your day holds for you . . . with a satisfied feeling and a smile.

Right:
Cheesy Chicken Ranch Sandwich (recipe on page 246)

Cheesy Spinach Burgers

1 envelope LIPTON® RECIPE SECRETS® Garlic Mushroom Soup Mix*
2 pounds ground beef
1 package (10 ounces) frozen chopped spinach, thawed and squeezed dry
1 cup shredded mozzarella or Cheddar cheese (about 4 ounces)

*Also terrific with LIPTON® RECIPE SECRETS® Onion Soup Mix.

1. In large bowl, combine all ingredients; shape into 8 patties.

2. Grill or broil until done. Serve, if desired, on hamburger buns.

Makes 8 servings

Recipe Tip: LIPTON ONION BUTTER makes a terrific topping for vegetables, potatoes, hot bread or rolls. Thoroughly blend 1 envelope LIPTON® RECIPE SECRETS® Onion Soup Mix with ¾ cup softened butter or margarine. Store covered in the refrigerator. Makes 1 cup.

Huevos Ranchwich

Prep Time: *10 minutes*   **Cook Time:** *5 minutes*

¼ cup EGG BEATERS® Healthy Real Egg Product
1 teaspoon diced green chiles
1 whole wheat hamburger roll, split and toasted
1 tablespoon thick and chunky salsa, heated
1 tablespoon shredded reduced-fat Cheddar and Monterey Jack cheese blend

On lightly greased griddle or skillet, pour Egg Beaters® into lightly greased 4-inch egg ring or biscuit cutter. Sprinkle with chiles. Cook 2 to 3 minutes or until bottom of egg patty is set. Remove egg ring and turn egg patty over. Cook 1 to 2 minutes longer or until done.

To serve, place egg patty on bottom half of roll. Top with salsa, cheese and roll top.

Makes 1 sandwich

Quick Tip

Oven broiling and grilling are suitable for thin cuts of meat, such as burgers, steaks and chops. Preheat the broiler or prepare the grill for direct grilling. Place the meat on the rack of the broiler pan so that fat can drip off during cooking.

Right:
Cheesy Spinach Burger

Peanut Pitas

  1 package (8 ounces) small pita breads, cut crosswise in half
16 teaspoons reduced-fat peanut butter
16 teaspoons strawberry spreadable fruit
  1 large banana, peeled and thinly sliced (about 48 slices)

1. Spread inside of each pita half with 1 teaspoon each peanut butter and spreadable fruit.

2. Fill pita halves evenly with banana slices. Serve immediately.

Makes 8 servings

Honey Bees: Substitute honey for spreadable fruit.

Jolly Jellies: Substitute any flavor jelly for spreadable fruit and thin apple slices for banana slices.

P. B. Crunchers: Substitute reduced fat mayonnaise for spreadable fruit and celery slices for banana slices.

Right:
Peanut Pitas

Brunch Sandwiches

Prep Time: 5 *minutes*   **Cook Time:** 10 *minutes*

4 English muffins, split, lightly toasted
8 thin slices HORMEL® Cure 81 ham
8 teaspoons Dijon mustard
8 large eggs, fried or poached
8 slices SARGENTO® Deli Style Sliced Swiss Cheese

1. Top each muffin half with a slice of ham, folding to fit. Spread mustard lightly over ham; top with an egg and one slice cheese.

2. Transfer to foil-lined baking sheet. Broil 4 to 5 inches from heat source until cheese is melted and sandwiches are hot, 2 to 3 minutes.

Makes 4 servings

Hickory Pork Tenderloin with Apple Topping

1 ¼ cups plus 2 tablespoons LAWRY'S® Hickory Marinade with Apple Cider, divided
1 pork tenderloin (2½-3 pounds)
1 can (1 pound 5 ounces) apple pie filling or topping

In large resealable plastic food storage bag, combine 1 cup Hickory Marinade and tenderloin; seal bag. Marinate in refrigerator at least 30 minutes. Remove tenderloin; discard used marinade. Grill tenderloin, using indirect heat method, 35 minutes or until no longer pink in center, turning once and basting often with additional ¼ cup Hickory Marinade. Let stand 10 minutes before slicing. In medium saucepan, combine additional 2 tablespoons Hickory Marinade and apple pie filling. Cook over low heat until heated throughout. Spoon over tenderloin slices. *Makes 6 to 8 servings*

Serving Suggestion: Serve with Brussels sprouts and cornbread. Garnish with cranberries, if desired.

Hint: Various flavored applesauces can be substituted for the apple pie filling. Try chunky applesauce with brown sugar and cinnamon.

Right:
Hickory Pork Tenderloin with Apple Topping

Baked Eggs

4 eggs
4 teaspoons milk
   Salt and black pepper to taste

1. Preheat oven to 375°F. Grease 4 small baking dishes or custard cups.

2. Break 1 egg into each dish. Add 1 teaspoon milk to each dish. Season with salt and pepper.

3. Bake about 15 minutes or until set.   *Makes 4 servings*

Baked Egg Options: Top eggs with desired amount of one or more of the following before baking: light cream, salsa, shredded cheese, chopped ham, minced chives or minced fresh herbs. Bake as directed above.

Campbell's® Quick Beef 'n' Beans Tacos
Prep Time: 15 *minutes*   **Cook Time:** 10 *minutes*

   1 pound ground beef
   1 small onion, chopped (about ¼ cup)
   1 can (11¼ ounces) CAMPBELL'S® Condensed Fiesta Chili Beef Soup
¼ cup water
10 taco shells
   Shredded Cheddar cheese, shredded lettuce, diced tomato and sour cream

1. In medium skillet over medium-high heat, cook beef and onion until beef is browned, stirring to separate meat. Pour off fat.

2. Add soup and water. Reduce heat to low. Cover and cook 5 minutes.

3. Divide meat mixture among taco shells. Top with cheese, lettuce, tomato and sour cream.   *Makes 10 tacos*

Quick Tip

Use a microwave oven to quickly warm taco shells. Place 8 crisp taco shells on a paper towel. Heat at HIGH 20 to 30 seconds or just until warm; spoon in filling. To warm 1 or 2 taco shells, heat at HIGH 10 to 15 seconds.

Right:
Baked Egg

Wild Wedges

2 (8-inch) fat-free flour tortillas
   Nonstick cooking spray
⅓ cup shredded reduced-fat Cheddar cheese
⅓ cup chopped cooked chicken or turkey
 1 green onion, thinly sliced (about ¼ cup)
 2 tablespoons mild, thick and chunky salsa

1. Heat large nonstick skillet over medium heat until hot.

2. Spray one side of one flour tortilla with nonstick cooking spray; place sprayed side down in skillet. Top with cheese, chicken, green onion and salsa. Place remaining tortilla over mixture; spray with nonstick cooking spray.

3. Cook 2 to 3 minutes per side or until golden brown and cheese is melted. Cut into 8 triangles.   *Makes 4 servings*

Variation: For bean quesadillas, omit the chicken and spread ⅓ cup canned fat-free refried beans over one of the tortillas.

Right:
Wild Wedges

Cheesy Chicken Ranch Sandwiches

Prep Time: *5 minutes*   **Broil Time:** *14 minutes*

6 boneless skinless chicken breast halves (about 2 pounds)
²/₃ cup KRAFT® Ranch Dressing, divided
½ pound (8 ounces) VELVEETA® Pasteurized Prepared Cheese Product, sliced
6 French bread rolls, split
Lettuce

1. Brush chicken with ⅓ cup of the dressing. Spray rack of broiler pan with no stick cooking spray. Place chicken on rack of broiler pan.

2. Broil 3 to 4 inches from heat 5 to 6 minutes on each side or until cooked through. Top chicken with Velveeta. Broil an additional 2 minutes or until Velveeta is melted.

3. Spread rolls with remaining dressing; fill with lettuce and chicken.

Makes 6 sandwiches

Use Your Grill: Prepare chicken as directed. Grill over hot coals 5 to 6 minutes on each side or until cooked through. Top with Velveeta and continue grilling until Velveeta is melted. Continue as directed.

Campbell's® Italian Burger Melt

Prep and Cook Time: *20 minutes*

1 pound ground beef
1 can (11 ⅛ ounces) CAMPBELL'S® Condensed Italian Tomato Soup
¼ cup water
4 slices mozzarella, process American *or* Monterey Jack cheese (about 4 ounces)
4 hamburger rolls, split and toasted

1. Shape beef into 4 patties, ½ inch thick.

2. In medium skillet over medium-high heat, cook patties until browned. Set patties aside. Pour off fat.

3. Add soup and water. Heat to a boil. Return patties to skillet. Reduce heat to low. Cover and cook 10 minutes or until patties are no longer pink (160°F.).

4. Place cheese on patties and cook until cheese is melted. Place patties on 4 roll halves. Top with soup mixture and remaining roll halves.   *Makes 4 sandwiches*

Serving Idea: Serve with **Swanson Simple Seasoned Pasta**. In medium saucepan over medium-high heat, heat to a boil 2 cans (14½ ounces *each*) SWANSON® Seasoned Chicken Broth with Italian Herbs. Stir in 3 cups *uncooked* corkscrew pasta. Reduce heat to medium. Simmer gently 10 minutes or until pasta is done, stirring occasionally. Serves about 6.

Smart Tip

To meet USDA standards, all ground beef must be at least 70 percent lean. Ground chuck contains more fat and therefore produces juicier burgers. If you are not sure what to buy, ask your butcher.

Tuna Mac

Prep Time: 10 *minutes*   **Cook Time:** 15 *minutes*

2 cups water
2 cups (8 ounces) elbow macaroni, uncooked
¾ pound (12 ounces) VELVEETA® Pasteurized Prepared Cheese Product,
  cut up
1 package (16 ounces) frozen vegetable blend, thawed, drained
1 can (6 ounces) tuna, drained, flaked
2 tablespoons milk

1. Bring water to boil in saucepan. Stir in macaroni. Reduce heat to medium-low; cover. Simmer 8 to 10 minutes or until macaroni is tender.

2. Add Velveeta, vegetables, tuna and milk; stir until Velveeta is melted.

Makes 4 to 6 servings

A Taste of Nutrition: With mixed vegetables, Tuna Mac is an excellent source of vitamin A. But you can also substitute any 16-ounce package of a frozen vegetable for the mixed vegetable blend if your family has a particular favorite.

Right:
Tuna Mac

Quick Tip

To quickly shred a cabbage, first core it and cut it into quarters. Place a quarter, flat side down, on cutting board. Thinly slice the cabbage crosswise into shreds, using a stainless steel chef's knife or utility knife. (Cabbage pigment can react with a carbon steel blade and turn the leaves an unappetizing blue color.)

Right:
Bratwurst Skillet Breakfast

Bratwurst Skillet Breakfast

Prep and Cook Time: 30 *minutes*

1 ½ **pounds red potatoes**
    3 **bratwurst links (about ¾ pound)**
    2 **tablespoons butter or margarine**
1 ½ **teaspoons caraway seeds**
    4 **cups shredded red cabbage**

1. Cut potatoes into ¼- to ½-inch pieces. Place in microwavable casserole. Microwave, covered, at HIGH 3 minutes; stir. Microwave 2 minutes more or until just fork-tender; set aside.

2. While potatoes are cooking, slice bratwurst into ¼-inch pieces. Place in large skillet. Cook over medium-high heat. Cook, stirring occasionally, 8 minutes or until browned and no longer pink in center. Remove bratwurst from pan with slotted spoon; set aside. Pour off drippings.

3. Melt butter in skillet. Add potatoes and caraway seeds. Cook, stirring occasionally, 6 to 8 minutes or until potatoes are golden and tender. Return bratwurst to skillet; stir in cabbage. Cook, covered, 3 minutes or until cabbage is slightly wilted. Uncover and stir 3 to 4 minutes more or until cabbage is just tender yet still bright red. Serve with fresh fruit, if desired.   *Makes 4 servings*

Savory Salmon

6 small salmon steaks (about 6 ounces *each*)
¾ cup prepared HIDDEN VALLEY® Original Ranch® Salad Dressing
2 teaspoons chopped fresh dill *or* ¼ teaspoon dried dill weed
1 teaspoon chopped fresh parsley
  Lemon wedges
  Fresh dill sprigs (optional)

Preheat oven to 375°F. Arrange salmon in large buttered baking dish; spread 2 tablespoons salad dressing over each steak. Sprinkle with chopped dill and parsley. Bake until fish flakes easily when tested with fork, 10 to 15 minutes. Place under broiler 45 to 60 seconds to brown. Serve with lemon wedges and garnish with dill sprigs, if desired. *Makes 6 servings*

Pace® Baked Potatoes Olé
Prep Time: *5 minutes*   **Cook Time:** *15 minutes*

1 pound ground beef
1 tablespoon chili powder
1 cup PACE® Picante Sauce *or* Thick & Chunky Salsa
4 hot baked potatoes, split
  Shredded Cheddar cheese

1. In medium skillet over medium-high heat, cook beef and chili powder until beef is browned, stirring to separate meat. Pour off fat.

2. Add picante sauce. Reduce heat to low and heat through. Serve over potatoes. Top with cheese. *Makes 4 servings*

Right:
Savory Salmon

Wisconsin Cheese Stuffed Burgers

3 pounds ground beef
¹/₂ cup dry bread crumbs
2 eggs
1 ¹/₄ cups (5 ounces) of your favorite shredded Wisconsin cheese, shredded, such as Pepper Havarti cheese, crumbled Blue cheese or crumbled Basil & Tomato Feta cheese

In a large mixing bowl, combine beef, bread crumbs and eggs; mix well, but lightly. Divide mixture into 24 balls; flatten each on waxed paper to 4 inches across. Place 1 tablespoon cheese on each of 12 patties. Top with remaining patties, carefully pressing edges to seal. Grill patties 4 inches from coals, turning only once, 6 to 9 minutes on each side or until no longer pink. To keep cheese between patties as it melts, do not flatten burgers with spatula while grilling.

Makes 12 servings

CAUTION: Cheese filling may be very hot if eaten immediately after cooking.

Favorite recipe from **Wisconsin Milk Marketing Board**

Campbell's® Quick Turkey Quesadillas

Prep Time: 10 *minutes*   **Cook Time:** 15 *minutes*

1 can (10³/₄ ounces) CAMPBELL'S® Condensed Cheddar Cheese Soup
¹/₂ cup PACE® Thick & Chunky Salsa *or* Picante Sauce (Medium)
2 cups cubed cooked turkey
10 flour tortillas (8-inch)
Fiesta Rice (optional, recipe follows)

1. Preheat oven to 425°F.

2. In medium saucepan mix soup, salsa and turkey. Over medium heat, heat through, stirring often.

3. Place tortillas on 2 baking sheets. Top **half** of each tortilla with $\frac{1}{3}$ **cup** soup mixture. Spread to within $\frac{1}{2}$ inch of edge. Moisten edges of tortilla with water. Fold over and press edges together.

4. Bake 5 minutes or until hot. Serve with Fiesta Rice, if desired.   *Makes 4 servings*

Fiesta Rice: In medium saucepan, mix 1 can ($10\frac{1}{2}$ ounces) CAMPBELL'S® Condensed Chicken Broth, $\frac{1}{2}$ cup water and $\frac{1}{2}$ cup PACE® Thick & Chunky Salsa. Over medium-high heat, heat to a boil. Stir in 2 cups uncooked Minute® Original Rice. Cover and remove from heat. Let stand 5 minutes. Fluff with fork. Makes 4 servings.

Chicken Thighs with Ginger-Lime Marinade

$\frac{3}{4}$ **cup WISH-BONE® Italian Dressing**
2 tablespoons honey
4 teaspoons lime juice
1 teaspoon ground ginger
$\frac{1}{4}$ **teaspoon crushed red pepper flakes (optional)**
6 medium chicken thighs (about 2 pounds)

For marinade, combine all ingredients except chicken. In large, shallow nonaluminum baking dish or plastic bag, add chicken and $\frac{3}{4}$ cup of the marinade; turn to coat. Cover, or close bag, and marinate in refrigerator, turning occasionally, 3 to 24 hours. Refrigerate remaining marinade.

Remove chicken, discarding marinade. Grill or broil chicken, turning once and brushing frequently with refrigerated marinade, until chicken is done.

Makes 4 servings

Campbell's® French Onion Burgers

Prep and Cook Time: 20 *minutes*

1 pound ground beef
1 can (10½ ounces) CAMPBELL'S® Condensed French Onion Soup
4 round hard rolls, split
4 slices cheese (use your favorite)

1. Shape beef into 4 patties, ½ inch thick.

2. In medium skillet over medium-high heat, cook patties until browned. Set patties aside. Pour off fat.

3. Add soup. Heat to a boil. Return patties to skillet. Reduce heat to low. Cover and cook 10 minutes or until patties are no longer pink (160°F.).

4. Place cheese on patties and cook until cheese is melted. Place patties on 4 roll halves. Top with remaining roll halves. Serve with soup mixture for dipping.

Makes 4 sandwiches

Right (top to bottom): *Campbell's® French Onion Burger and Campbell's® Italian Burger Melt (page 247)*

Eggstra Special Omelets for Two

6 eggs
3 tablespoons half and half, light cream or milk
¼ teaspoon salt
⅛ teaspoon ground black pepper
2 tablespoons I CAN'T BELIEVE IT'S NOT BUTTER!® Spread, divided

In small bowl, with wire whisk or fork, beat eggs, half and half, salt and pepper; set aside.

In 8-inch nonstick skillet, melt 1 tablespoon I Can't Believe It's Not Butter! Spread and add ½ of the egg mixture. With spatula, lift set edges of omelet, tilting pan to allow uncooked mixture to flow to bottom. When omelet is set and slightly moist, add desired Special Omelet Filling. With spatula, fold omelet and cook an additional 30 seconds. Repeat with remaining 1 tablespoon I Can't Believe It's Not Butter! Spread and egg mixture. *Makes 2 servings*

Special Omelet Fillings:
Springtime Asparagus Omelet: In 10-inch skillet, melt 2 tablespoons I CAN'T BELIEVE IT'S NOT BUTTER!® Spread over medium-high heat and cook ¼ cup chopped shallots or onions until tender. Add 1½ cups cut-up asparagus and salt and ground black pepper to taste. Cook until asparagus is tender. Spoon into omelets, then evenly sprinkle with ¼ cup grated Parmesan cheese.

Western Omelet: In 10-inch skillet, melt 1 tablespoon I CAN'T BELIEVE IT'S NOT BUTTER!® Spread over medium-high heat and cook 1 cup chopped bell pepper, 1 cup diced potatoes, ½ cup chopped onion, and salt and ground black pepper to taste, stirring occasionally, until vegetables are tender. Spoon into omelets.

Fresh Tomato-Basil Omelet: Fill omelets with 2 chopped plum tomatoes, ⅔ cup chopped fresh mozzarella cheese, 4 fresh basil leaves, cut into thin strips, and salt and ground black pepper to taste.

Right:
*Eggstra Special
Omelet for Two*

Veg•All® Pita Pockets

1 can (15 ounces) VEG•ALL® Original Mixed Vegetables, drained
1 can (10 ounces) water-packed chunk-style chicken, drained
½ cup shredded cheddar or Swiss cheese
⅓ cup ranch or other creamy salad dressing
2 pita bread rounds
4 large lettuce leaves

In medium bowl, combine Veg•All, chicken, cheese and salad dressing. Cut pita bread rounds in half. Carefully open bread. Place 1 lettuce leaf in each pocket. Stuff each pocket with chicken mixture, divided evenly. *Makes 4 servings*

Warm Steak Salad

1 beef flank steak (about 1¼ pounds)
Salt and pepper
¼ pound sugar snap peas or snow peas
Lettuce leaves
1 medium red onion, sliced, separated into rings
1 pint cherry tomatoes
Prepared honey mustard dressing (optional)

1. Preheat broiler. Position oven rack about 4 inches from heat source. Place steak on rack of broiler pan. Broil 10 minutes or to desired doneness, turning after 5 minutes. Season with salt and pepper to taste.

2. Meanwhile, bring lightly salted water to a boil in medium saucepan. Add peas; cook 2 minutes. Drain. Place steak on cutting board. Cut diagonally, across grain of meat, into thin slices.

3. Line serving platter with lettuce. Arrange steak slices in center of platter. Surround with onion rings, snow peas and cherry tomatoes. Serve with dressing, if desired. *Makes 4 servings*

Right:
Veg•All® Pita Pockets

Baked Cod with Tomatoes and Olives
Prep and Cook Time: 25 minutes

1 pound cod fillets (about 4 fillets), cut into 2-inch pieces
1 can (14½ ounces) diced Italian-style tomatoes, drained
2 tablespoons chopped pitted ripe olives
1 teaspoon bottled minced garlic
2 tablespoons chopped fresh parsley

1. Preheat oven to 400°F. Spray 13×9-inch baking dish with nonstick olive oil-flavored cooking spray. Arrange cod fillets in pan; season to taste with salt and pepper.

2. Combine tomatoes, olives and garlic in medium bowl. Spoon over fish.

3. Bake 20 minutes or until fish flakes when tested with a fork. Sprinkle with parsley.   *Makes 4 servings*

Serving Tip

To add color and flavor to almost any meal, spread split French bread with softened butter, sprinkle with paprika and dried oregano leaves, and broil until lightly toasted.

Reuben Roll-Ups
Prep Time: 20 minutes   **Cook Time:** 10 minutes

8 (7-inch) flour tortillas
¾ cup French's® Hearty Deli Brown Mustard
1 pound sliced corned beef
2 cups (8 ounces) shredded Swiss cheese
½ cup sauerkraut

Spread each tortilla with about 1½ tablespoons mustard. Layer corned beef, cheese and sauerkraut on tortillas, dividing evenly. Roll up tortillas jelly-roll style. Secure with toothpicks.*

Place tortillas on oiled barbecue grill grid. Grill over medium-low coals about 10 minutes or until tortillas are toasted and cheese begins to melt, turning often. Remove toothpicks before serving.   *Makes 4 servings*

Soak toothpicks in water 20 minutes first to prevent burning.

*Right:
Baked Cod with Tomatoes and Olives*

Caramelized Onion, Brie & Smoked Ham Croissants

¼ cup I CAN'T BELIEVE IT'S NOT BUTTER!® Spread
1 large Spanish onion, thinly sliced
8 slices Canadian bacon (about 4 ounces)
4 large heated croissants, halved lengthwise, or bagels, split and toasted
8 ounces Brie cheese, cut into ⅛-inch wedges

Preheat oven to 350°F.

In 12-inch skillet, melt I Can't Believe It's Not Butter! Spread over medium-high heat and cook onion, stirring occasionally, 10 minutes or until golden brown. Remove onion and set aside.

In same skillet, heat bacon, turning once.

On baking sheet, arrange 4 croissant halves. Evenly top with bacon, then onions, then cheese. Bake 2 minutes or until cheese is slightly melted. Top with remaining croissant halves and serve hot.   *Makes 4 servings*

Right:
*Carmelized Onion,
Brie & Smoked
Ham Croissant*

Garlic Roast Beef Subs

Prep Time: 10 *minutes*   **Cook Time:** *about* 10 *minutes*

  2 cups thinly sliced onions
  3 tablespoons *French's*® Worcestershire Sauce
  1 container (4 ounces) garlic-flavored cheese spread
  4 sandwich rolls, split in half and toasted
12 ounces sliced deli roast beef

1. Melt 1 *tablespoon butter* in medium skillet over medium-high heat. Add onions; cook and stir 5 minutes or until tender. Add Worcestershire; cook 2 minutes.

2. Spread about 1 *tablespoon* cheese on each half of rolls. Broil 30 seconds or until cheese begins to brown. Layer roast beef and onions on bottoms of rolls. Cover with top halves.

Makes 4 servings

Wilted Spinach Salad

¼ pound diced bacon
½ pound fresh spinach leaves, washed, drained and torn
 2 hard-cooked eggs, sliced
 2 tomatoes, cut into wedges
 1 cup prepared HIDDEN VALLEY® Original Ranch® Salad Dressing & Recipe Mix

In skillet, fry bacon until crispy; drain on paper towels. Reserve drippings. Place spinach in salad bowl; arrange bacon, eggs and tomatoes on top. Heat bacon drippings until hot; stir in salad dressing and cook until warmed. Pour over salad.

Makes 4 to 6 servings

Smart Tip

To check if an egg has been hard-cooked, spin it like a top. If it spins on its end, it is cooked; if it turns on its side, it is raw.

Right:
Garlic Roast Beef Sub

Chili-Cheese Quesadillas

2 tablespoons part-skim ricotta cheese
6 (6-inch) corn tortillas
½ cup (2 ounces) shredded reduced-fat Monterey Jack cheese
2 tablespoons diced mild green chilies
 Nonstick cooking spray
 Salsa Cruda (optional, page 186, or prepared salsa)

1. To make 1 quesadilla, spread 2 teaspoons ricotta over tortilla. Sprinkle with heaping tablespoonful Monterey Jack cheese and 2 teaspoons diced chilies. Top with 1 tortilla. Repeat to make 2 more quesadillas.

2. Spray small nonstick skillet with cooking spray. Heat over medium-high heat. Add 1 quesadilla; cook 2 minutes or until bottom is golden. Turn quesadilla over; cook 2 minutes. Remove from heat. Cut into 4 wedges. Repeat with remaining quesadillas. Serve warm with Salsa Cruda, if desired. *Makes 4 servings*

Campbell's® Saucy Pork Chops
Prep and Cook Time: 15 *minutes*

1 tablespoon vegetable oil
4 pork chops, ½ inch thick (about 1 pound)
1 can (10¾ ounces) CAMPBELL'S® Condensed Cream of Onion Soup
¼ cup water

1. In medium skillet over medium-high heat, heat oil. Add chops and cook 8 minutes or until browned. Set chops aside. Pour off fat.

2. Add soup and water. Heat to a boil. Return chops to pan. Reduce heat to low. Cover and cook 5 minutes or until chops are no longer pink. *Makes 4 servings*

Right:
*Chili-Cheese
Quesadillas*

Cheddar Cheesesteak Sandwiches

Prep Time: 5 *minutes*   **Cook Time:** 10 *minutes*

2 tablespoons margarine or butter
1 large onion, thinly sliced
6 all-beef fresh or frozen sandwich steaks
1 jar (16 ounces) RAGÚ® Cheese Creations!® Double Cheddar Sauce
6 hero or sandwich rolls

1. In 12-inch skillet, melt margarine over medium heat and cook onion, covered, stirring occasionally, 4 minutes or until tender. Remove onion and set aside. In same skillet, cook steaks 2 minutes or until done.

2. In 3-quart saucepan, heat Ragú Cheese Creations! Sauce. Arrange steaks and onions in rolls; top with hot sauce.   *Makes 6 servings*

Fish in Foil

1 (8-ounce) can stewed tomatoes
⅓ cup A.1.® BOLD & SPICY Steak Sauce
1 clove garlic, minced
4 (4-ounce) firm fish fillets
2 cups frozen mixed vegetables

In small bowl, combine stewed tomatoes, steak sauce and garlic; set aside.

Place each fish fillet in center of heavy duty or double-thickness foil; top each with ½ cup mixed vegetables and ¼ cup steak sauce mixture. Wrap foil securely.

Grill fish packets over medium heat for 8 to 10 minutes or until fish flakes easily with fork. Serve immediately.   *Makes 4 servings*

Right:
*Cheddar
Cheesesteak
Sandwich*

Bread

Right:
Anadama Bread
*(recipe on page
278)*

There's only one thing better than the aroma of homemade bread,

and that's being able to make it quickly and easily. Enjoy these

effortless recipes, whether creating wondrous wake-up muffins and

sweet treats, or making your own savory loaves to accompany an

exciting entrée. You'll probably end up eating the breads by

themselves!

Berry Filled Muffins

1 package DUNCAN HINES® Blueberry Muffin Mix
1 egg
½ cup water
¼ cup strawberry jam
2 tablespoons sliced natural almonds

1. Preheat oven to 400°F. Place 8 (2½-inch) paper or foil liners in muffin cups; set aside.

2. Rinse blueberries from Mix with cold water and drain.

3. Empty muffin mix into bowl. Break up any lumps. Add egg and water. Stir until moistened, about 50 strokes. Fill cups half full with batter.

4. Fold blueberries into jam. Spoon on top of batter in each cup. Spread gently. Cover with remaining batter. Sprinkle with almonds. Bake at 400°F for 17 to 20 minutes or until set and golden brown. Cool in pan 5 to 10 minutes. Loosen carefully before removing from pan.   *Makes 8 muffins*

Tip: For a delicious flavor variation, try using blackberry or red raspberry jam instead of the strawberry jam.

Right:
*Berry Filled
Muffins*

Crispy Ranch Breadsticks

2 tablespoons dry ranch party dip mix
2 tablespoons sour cream
1 package (10 ounces) refrigerated pizza dough
  Butter, melted

1. Preheat oven to 400°F. Grease baking sheets or line with parchment paper. Combine dip mix and sour cream in small bowl; set aside.

2. Unroll pizza dough on lightly floured work surface. Shape dough into 16×10-inch rectangle. Brush with melted butter. Spread dip mixture evenly over top of dough; cut into 24 (10-inch) strips. Shape into desired shapes.

3. Place breadsticks ½ inch apart on prepared baking sheets. Bake 10 minutes or until golden brown. Serve immediately or place on wire rack to cool.

Makes 24 breadsticks

Biscuits

2 cups sifted all-purpose flour
3 teaspoons baking powder
1 teaspoon salt
⅓ CRISCO® Stick or ⅓ cup CRISCO® all-vegetable shortening
¾ cup milk

1. Heat oven to 425°F. Combine flour, baking powder and salt in bowl. Cut in ⅓ cup shortening using pastry blender (or 2 knives) until mixture resembles coarse meal. Add milk; stir with fork until blended.

2. Transfer dough to lightly floured surface. Knead gently 8 to 10 times. Roll dough ½ inch thick. Cut with floured 2-inch-round cutter.

3. Bake at 425°F 12 to 15 minutes. *Do not overbake.*

Makes 12 to 16 (2-inch) biscuits

Smart Tip

Parchment is heavy paper that is impervious to grease and moisture. It is sold in sheets and in rolls. There are many uses for it in the kitchen, including lining baking sheets for cookies, meringues and cream puffs. It allows for easy removal of baked goods.

Right:
Crispy Ranch Breadsticks

Anadama Bread

7³⁄₄ to 8¹⁄₄ cups all-purpose flour, divided
2 packages (¹⁄₄ ounce each) active dry yeast
1¹⁄₂ teaspoons salt
2³⁄₄ cups water
³⁄₄ cup molasses
¹⁄₄ cup butter or margarine
1¹⁄₄ cups yellow cornmeal

1. Combine 4 cups flour, yeast and salt in large bowl. Combine water, molasses and butter in 2-quart saucepan. Heat over low heat until mixture is 120° to 130°F. (Butter does not need to completely melt.) Gradually beat water mixture into flour mixture with electric mixer at low speed. Increase speed to medium; beat 2 minutes. Beat in cornmeal and 2 cups flour at low speed. Increase speed to medium; beat 2 minutes.

2. Stir in enough additional flour, about 1³⁄₄ cups, to make soft dough. Turn out dough onto floured surface; flatten slightly. Knead dough 8 to 10 minutes or until smooth and elastic, adding remaining ¹⁄₂ cup flour to prevent sticking, if necessary. Shape dough into a ball; place in large greased bowl. Turn dough over so that top is greased. Cover with towel; let rise in warm place about 1 hour or until doubled in bulk.

3. Punch down dough. Knead dough on well-floured surface 1 minute. Cut dough into halves. Cover with towel; let rest 10 minutes. Grease 2 (1¹⁄₂-quart) soufflé or casserole dishes or 2 (9×5-inch) loaf pans. For soufflé dishes, shape each half of dough into a ball; place in greased pans. For loaf pans, roll out one half of dough into 12×8-inch rectangle with well-floured rolling pin. Starting with one 8-inch side, roll up dough jelly-roll style. Pinch seam and ends to seal. Place loaf, seam side down, in prepared pan, tucking ends under. Repeat with remaining dough. Cover and let rise in warm place about 40 minutes or until doubled in bulk.

4. Preheat oven to 375°F. Bake 35 to 40 minutes or until loaves are browned and sound hollow when tapped. Quickly remove from soufflé dishes; cool on wire racks.

Makes 2 loaves

Basic Yeast Bread

- 1 cup milk
- 1 teaspoon salt
- 1 egg
- 2 tablespoons unsalted butter, softened
- 3¼ cups all-purpose bread flour
- 1 tablespoon sugar
- 2 teaspoons active dry yeast

Measure all ingredients carefully; place in bread machine pan in order specified by owner's manual. Program dough cycle setting; press start.

Makes 2 loaves

Savory Pull-Apart Loaf: Prepare Basic Yeast Bread dough as instructed. Grease 9×5-inch loaf pan; set aside. Combine 1 tablespoon *each* dried basil, thyme and rubbed sage in small bowl; set aside. Turn out dough onto lightly floured work surface. Divide dough into 16 equal pieces. Form each piece into ball. Cover with clean towel; let rest 5 minutes.

Flatten each ball into 4×3-inch oval. Lightly coat both sides of dough with olive oil. Sprinkle one side of each dough oval with rounded ½ teaspoon herb mixture. Stand loaf pan on short end. Lay one piece of dough, herb-covered side down, in pan. Stack remaining 15 pieces of dough in pan so that herb-covered sides of dough are touching sides of dough not covered with herb mixture. Cover with towel; let rise in warm place 45 minutes.

Preheat oven to 375°F. Bake 35 minutes or until top of loaf is golden. Immediately remove bread from pan and cool on wire rack. Makes 1 loaf.

Above:
Savory Pull-Apart Loaf

Fast Pesto Focaccia

Prep and Cook Time: 20 *minutes*

1 can (10 ounces) pizza crust dough
2 tablespoons prepared pesto
4 sun-dried tomatoes packed in oil, drained

1. Preheat oven to 425°F. Lightly grease 8×8×2-inch pan. Unroll pizza dough; fold in half and pat into pan.

2. Spread pesto evenly over dough. Chop tomatoes or snip with kitchen scissors; sprinkle over pesto. Press tomatoes into dough. Make indentations in dough every 2 inches using wooden spoon handle.

3. Bake 10 to 12 minutes or until golden brown. Cut into squares and serve warm or at room temperature.

Makes 16 appetizers

Mexican Corn Bread

Prep time: 10 *minutes*   **Cook time:** 20 *minutes*

¼ pound VELVEETA® Mexican Pasteurized Process Cheese Spread with
    Jalapeño Peppers, cubed
2 tablespoons milk
1 egg, beaten
1 (8½-ounce) package corn muffin mix

• Preheat oven to 350°F.

• Stir together process cheese spread and milk in saucepan over low heat until process cheese spread is melted. Add with egg to muffin mix, mixing just until moistened. Pour into greased 8-inch square pan.

• Bake 20 minutes   *Makes 6 to 8 servings*

Variation: Substitute VELVEETA® Pasteurized Prepared Cheese Product for VELVEETA® Pasteurized Process Cheese Spread with Jalapeño Peppers.

Right:
Fast Pesto Focaccia

Blueberry Orange Muffins

   1 **package DUNCAN HINES® Blueberry Muffin Mix**
   2 **egg whites**
  ½ **cup orange juice**
   1 **teaspoon grated orange peel**

1. Preheat oven to 400°F. Grease 2½-inch muffin cups (or use paper liners).

2. Rinse blueberries from Mix with cold water and drain.

3. Empty muffin mix into large bowl. Break up any lumps. Add egg whites, orange juice and orange peel. Stir until moistened, about 50 strokes. Fold blueberries gently into batter.

4. For large muffins, fill cups two-thirds full. Bake at 400°F 18 to 21 minutes or until toothpick inserted in center comes out clean. (For medium muffins, fill cups half full. Bake at 400°F 16 to 19 minutes or until toothpick inserted in center comes out clean.) Cool in pan 5 to 10 minutes. Carefully loosen muffins from pan. Remove to cooling racks. Serve warm or cool completely.

Makes 8 large or 12 medium muffins

Tip: Freeze extra grated orange peel for future use.

Kikko-Style French Rolls

   4 **tablespoons butter or margarine**
   1 **tablespoon KIKKOMAN® Teriyaki Marinade & Sauce**
  ¼ **teaspoon garlic powder**
   4 **French rolls**

Combine butter, teriyaki sauce and garlic powder in small saucepan with heatproof handle; heat on grill until butter melts. Slice each roll in half lengthwise. Place rolls, cut side down, on grill 3 to 4 inches from hot coals; cook about 2 minutes, or until golden brown. Brush butter mixture equally on each toasted roll half.

Makes 4 servings

Quick Tip

To quickly and easily fill muffin cups, place batter in a 4-cup glass measure. Fill each cup 3/4 full. Use a plastic spatula to control the flow of the batter.

Right:
Blueberry Orange Muffins

**Quick
Tip:**

*For a fast
start to your
day, prepare
cinnamon
buns or other
pastries, then
cover and
refrigerate
overnight.
Bake them in
the morning
for a quick,
delicious
treat.*

Cinnamon Bubble Ring

Prep and Cook Time: *30 minutes*

¼ **cup sugar**
½ **teaspoon ground cinnamon**
1 **can (11 ounces) refrigerated French bread dough**
1 ½ **tablespoons margarine or butter, melted**

1. Preheat oven to 350°F. Grease 9-inch tube pan. Combine sugar and cinnamon in small bowl.

2. Cut dough into 16 slices; roll into balls. Arrange 12 balls evenly spaced against outer wall of pan. Arrange remaining 4 balls evenly spaced against tube of pan. Brush with margarine. Sprinkle sugar mixture evenly over balls.

3. Bake 20 to 25 minutes or until golden brown. Serve warm.   *Makes 8 servings*

Gannat (French Cheese Bread)

3 **tablespoons water**
1 **teaspoon salt**
2 **eggs**
¼ **cup butter or margarine, cut up, softened**
2 ½ **cups all-purpose flour**
1 **teaspoon sugar**
1 **cup (4 ounces) shredded Cheddar or Swiss cheese**
2 **teaspoons active dry yeast**

1. Measure all ingredients carefully; place in bread machine pan in order specified by owner's manual.

2. Program basic or white cycle and desired crust setting; press start. *Do not use delay cycles.* Remove baked bread from pan; cool on wire rack.

Makes 1 (1½-pound) loaf (12 to 16 servings)

Right:
*Cinnamon Bubble
Ring*

Cranberry Cheesecake Muffins

Prep and Bake Time: 30 *minutes*

  1 package (3 ounces) cream cheese, softened
  4 tablespoons sugar, divided
  1 cup reduced-fat (2%) milk
⅓ cup vegetable oil
  1 egg
  1 package (about 15 ounces) cranberry quick bread mix

1. Preheat oven to 400°F. Grease 12 muffin cups.

2. Beat cream cheese and 2 tablespoons sugar in small bowl until well blended.

3. Beat milk, oil and egg in large bowl until blended. Stir in quick bread mix just until dry ingredients are moistened.

4. Fill muffin cups ¼ full with batter. Drop 1 teaspoon cream cheese mixture into center of each cup. Spoon remaining batter over cream cheese mixture.

5. Sprinkle batter with remaining 2 tablespoons sugar. Bake 17 to 22 minutes or until golden brown. Cool 5 minutes. Remove from muffin cups to wire rack to cool.

Makes 12 muffins

Above:
*Cranberry
Cheesecake Muffins*

Honey Cloverleafs

  1 package (16 ounces) hot roll mix
  6 tablespoons honey, divided
¼ cup butter or margarine
  1 teaspoon grated lemon peel
  1 cup sliced almonds

Prepare hot roll mix in large bowl according to package directions, adding 2 tablespoons honey to liquid. Cover kneaded dough with bowl and let rest 5 minutes.

Melt butter in small saucepan over medium heat. Add remaining 4 tablespoons honey; stir in lemon peel.

Roll dough into 36 balls (about 1- to 1½-inch diameter each). Form clusters of three balls; dip each cluster in honey mixture, then in almonds. Place each in well greased muffin cup. Cover and set in warm place to rise about 30 minutes or until doubled in bulk.

Bake in preheated 350°F oven 15 to 20 minutes or until lightly browned. Brush with remaining honey mixture, if desired. Remove from pan and cool slightly on wire rack. Serve warm or cool.

Makes 1 dozen rolls

Variation: Dough may be dipped in honey mixture then in chopped parsley, rosemary or other fresh herbs.

Favorite recipe from **National Honey Board**

Nutty Cinnamon Sticky Buns

Prep Time: 10 *minutes*   **Cook Time:** 25 *minutes*

- ⅓ **cup margarine or butter**
- ½ **cup packed brown sugar**
- ½ **cup PLANTERS® Pecans, chopped**
- 1 **teaspoon ground cinnamon**
- 1 **(17.3-ounce) package refrigerated biscuits (8 large biscuits)**

1. Melt margarine or butter in 9-inch round baking pan in 350°F oven.

2. Mix brown sugar, pecans and cinnamon in small bowl; sprinkle over melted margarine or butter in pan. Arrange biscuits in pan with sides touching (biscuits will fit tightly in pan).

3. Bake at 350°F for 25 to 30 minutes or until biscuits are golden brown and center biscuit is fully cooked. Invert pan immediately onto serving plate. Spread any remaining topping from pan on buns. Serve warm.

Makes 8 buns

Below:
Nutty Cinnamon Sticky Buns

Coconut Chocolate Chip Loaf

1 package DUNCAN HINES® Chocolate Chip Muffin Mix
1 1/3 cups toasted flaked coconut (see Tip below)
1 egg
3/4 cup water
1/2 teaspoon vanilla extract
Confectioners' sugar, for garnish (optional)

1. Preheat oven to 350°F. Grease and flour 9×5×3-inch loaf pan.

2. Empty muffin mix into medium bowl. Break up any lumps. Add coconut, egg, water and vanilla extract. Stir until moistened, about 50 strokes. Pour into pan. Bake at 350°F 45 to 50 minutes or until toothpick inserted in center comes out clean. Cool in pan 15 minutes. Invert onto cooling rack. Turn right side up. Cool completely. Dust with confectioners' sugar, if desired.   *Makes 1 loaf (12 slices)*

Tip: Spread coconut evenly on baking sheet. Toast at 350°F 5 minutes. Stir and toast 1 to 2 minutes longer or until light golden brown.

Country Recipe Biscuits

2 cups all-purpose flour
1 tablespoon baking powder
1/2 cup prepared HIDDEN VALLEY® Original Ranch® salad dressing
1/2 cup buttermilk

Preheat oven to 425°F. In small bowl, sift together flour and baking powder. Make a well in flour mixture; add salad dressing and buttermilk. Stir with fork until dough forms a ball. Drop by rounded spoonfuls onto ungreased baking sheet. Bake until lightly browned, 12 to 15 minutes.   *Makes 12 biscuits*

If a recipe calls for buttermilk and you have none, fresh milk can be soured and used as a substitute. For 1/2 cup of buttermilk, place 1 1/2 teaspoons lemon juice or distilled white vinegar in a measuring cup and add enough milk to measure 1/2 cup. Stir and let the mixture stand at room temperature for 5 minutes.

Right:
Coconut Chocolate Chip Loaf

Soft Pretzels

1 package (16 ounces) hot roll mix plus ingredients to prepare mix
1 egg white
2 teaspoons water
2 tablespoons *each* assorted coatings: grated Parmesan cheese, sesame seeds, poppy seeds, dried oregano leaves

1. Prepare hot roll mix according to package directions.

2. Preheat oven to 375°F. Spray baking sheets with nonstick cooking spray; set aside.

3. Divide dough equally into 16 pieces; roll each piece with hands to form a rope, 7 to 10 inches long. Place on prepared cookie sheets; form into desired shape (hearts, wreaths, pretzels, snails, loops, etc.).

4. Beat together egg white and water in small bowl until foamy. Brush onto dough shapes; sprinkle each shape with 1½ teaspoons of one of the coatings.

5. Bake until golden brown, about 15 minutes. Serve warm or at room temperature.

Makes 8 servings

Fruit Twists: Omit coatings. Prepare dough and roll into ropes as directed. Place ropes on lightly floured surface. Roll out, or pat, each rope into rectangle, ¼ inch thick; brush each rectangle with about 1 teaspoon spreadable fruit or preserves. Fold each rectangle lengthwise in half; twist into desired shape. Bake as directed.

Cheese Twists: Omit coatings. Prepare dough and roll into ropes as directed. Place ropes on lightly floured surface. Roll out, or pat, each rope into rectangle, ¼ inch thick. Sprinkle each rectangle with about 1 tablespoon shredded Cheddar or other flavor cheese. Fold each rectangle lengthwise in half; twist into desired shape. Bake as directed.

Right:
Soft Pretzels

Cinnamon Honey Buns

$\frac{1}{4}$ cup butter or margarine, softened and divided
$\frac{1}{2}$ cup honey, divided
$\frac{1}{4}$ cup chopped toasted nuts
2 teaspoons ground cinnamon
1 loaf (1 pound) frozen bread dough, thawed according to package directions
$\frac{2}{3}$ cup raisins

Grease 12 muffin cups with 1 tablespoon butter. To prepare honey-nut topping, mix together 1 tablespoon butter, $\frac{1}{4}$ cup honey and chopped nuts. Place 1 teaspoon topping in each muffin cup. To prepare filling, mix together remaining 2 tablespoons butter, remaining $\frac{1}{4}$ cup honey and cinnamon. Roll out bread dough onto floured surface into 18×8-inch rectangle. Spread filling evenly over dough. Sprinkle with raisins. Starting with long side, roll dough into log. Cut log into 12 (1$\frac{1}{2}$-inch) slices. Place 1 slice, cut side up, into each prepared muffin cup. Set muffin pan in warm place; let dough rise 30 minutes. Place muffin pan on foil-lined baking sheet. Bake at 375°F 20 minutes or until buns are golden brown. Remove from oven; cool in pan 5 minutes. Invert pan to remove buns.

Makes 12 buns

Favorite recipe from **National Honey Board**

Right:
Cinnamon Honey Buns

Crispy Onion Crescent Rolls

Prep Time: 15 *minutes*   **Cook Time:** 15 *minutes*

  1 can (8 ounces) refrigerated crescent dinner rolls
1 ⅓ cups French's® Taste Toppers™ French Fried Onions, slightly crushed
  1 egg, beaten

Preheat oven to 375°F. Line large baking sheet with foil. Separate refrigerated rolls into 8 triangles. Sprinkle center of each triangle with about 1½ tablespoons **Taste Toppers.** Roll-up triangles from short side, jelly-roll fashion. Sprinkle any excess **Taste Toppers** over top of crescents.

Arrange crescents on prepared baking sheet. Brush with beaten egg. Bake 15 minutes or until golden brown and crispy. Transfer to wire rack; cool slightly.

Makes 8 servings

Below:
Southern Biscuit Muffin

Right:
Crispy Onion Crescent Rolls

Southern Biscuit Muffins

2½ cups all-purpose flour
  ¼ cup sugar
1½ tablespoons baking powder
  ¾ cup cold butter
  1 cup cold milk

Preheat oven to 400°F. Grease 12 (2½-inch) muffin cups. (These muffins brown better on the sides and bottom when baked without paper liners.)

Combine flour, sugar and baking powder in large bowl. Cut in butter with pastry blender until mixture resembles coarse crumbs. Stir in milk just until flour mixture is moistened. Spoon evenly into prepared muffin cups.

Bake 20 minutes or until golden. Remove from pan. Cool on wire rack.

Makes 12 muffins

Tip: These muffins taste like baking powder biscuits and are very quick and easy to make. Serve them with jelly, jam or honey.

Cakes & Pies

Right:
Double Berry
Layer Cake (recipe
on page 316)

Win over your family with amazing cakes and pies that look and taste like they required hours to make, but only took minutes in the kitchen. Or, bring along one of these treats to a party or special event, and be assured it will be the center of attention on the dessert table.

Cherry-Topped Lemon Cheesecake Pie

Prep Time: *10 minutes*   **Chill Time:** *3 hours*

  1 (8-ounce) package cream cheese, softened
  1 (14-ounce) can EAGLE® BRAND Sweetened Condensed Milk (NOT
    evaporated milk)
  ⅓ cup REALEMON® Lemon Juice From Concentrate
  1 teaspoon vanilla extract
  1 (6-ounce) ready-made graham cracker crumb pie crust
  1 (21-ounce) can cherry pie filling, chilled

1. In large bowl, beat cream cheese until fluffy. Gradually beat in **Eagle Brand** until smooth. Stir in **ReaLemon** and vanilla. Pour into crust. Chill at least 3 hours.

2. To serve, top with cherry pie filling. Store covered in refrigerator.

Makes 6 to 8 servings

Note: For a firmer crust, brush crust with slightly beaten egg white; bake in 375°F oven 5 minutes. Cool before pouring filling into crust.

Pastel Party Pie

Prep Time: *10 minutes*   **Refrigerating Time:** *2½ hours*

  1¼ cups boiling water
    1 package (4-serving size) JELL-O® Brand Gelatin Dessert, any flavor
    1 pint (2 cups) ice cream (any flavor), softened
    1 prepared graham cracker crumb crust (6 ounces)

STIR boiling water into gelatin in large bowl at least 2 minutes until completely dissolved. Stir in ice cream until melted and smooth. Refrigerate 15 to 20 minutes or until mixture is very thick and will mound. Spoon into crust.

REFRIGERATE 2 hours or until firm.

Makes 8 servings

Quick Tip

If you forgot to remove ice cream from the freezer to soften it, here's how to soften it fast! Place a 1-pint container of hard-packed ice cream in a microwave oven and heat at MEDIUM (50% power) about 10 seconds or just until softened.

Right:
Cherry-Topped Lemon Cheesecake Pie

Lemonade Stand Pie

Prep time: *10 minutes*

1 can (6 ounces) frozen lemonade *or* pink lemonade concentrate,
   partially thawed
1 pint (2 cups) vanilla ice cream, softened
1 tub (8 ounces) COOL WHIP® Whipped Topping, thawed
1 prepared graham cracker crumb crust (6 ounces *or* 9 inches)

BEAT lemonade concentrate in large bowl with electric mixer on low speed about 30 seconds. Spoon in ice cream; beat until well blended. Gently stir in whipped topping until smooth. Freeze, if necessary, until mixture will mound. Spoon into crust.

FREEZE 4 hours or overnight. Let stand at room temperature 15 minutes or until pie can be cut easily. Garnish with additional whipped topping, lemon slices and fresh mint leaves, if desired.

Makes 8 servings

Frozen Strawberry-Yogurt Pie

2 containers (8 ounces each) vanilla or strawberry flavored yogurt
1 tub (8 ounces) COOL WHIP® Whipped Topping, thawed
2 cups sweetened strawberries, chopped
1 prepared graham cracker crumb crust (6 ounces)

STIR yogurt gently into whipped topping until well blended. Stir in strawberries. Spoon into crust.

FREEZE 4 hours or overnight until firm. Let stand in refrigerator 15 minutes or until pie can be cut easily.

GARNISH with additional whipped topping and whole strawberries, if desired. Store leftover pie in freezer.

Makes 8 servings

Quick Tip

For ease in serving crumb crust pie, dip pie plate just to rim in hot water 30 seconds to soften crust slightly. Cut and serve.

Right (clockwise from top): *Lemonade Stand Pie, Summer Lime Pie (page 308) and Frozen Strawberry-Yogurt Pie*

Light Banana Cream Pie
Prep time: 10 *minutes*   **Chill time:** 1 *hour*

    1 package (1.9 ounces) sugar-free vanilla instant pudding and pie filling
2¾ cups low fat milk
    4 ripe, medium DOLE® Bananas, sliced
    1 (9-inch) ready-made graham cracker pie crust
    1 firm, medium DOLE® Banana (optional)
    Light frozen non-dairy whipped topping, thawed (optional)

• **Prepare** pudding as directed, using 2¾ cups milk. Stir in sliced bananas.

• **Spoon** banana mixture into pie crust. Place plastic wrap over pie, lightly pressing plastic to completely cover filling. Chill 1 hour or until filling is set. Remove plastic wrap.

• **Cut** firm banana into ½-inch slices. Garnish pie with whipped topping and banana slices.
Makes 8 servings

Right:
*Light Banana
Cream Pie*

Chocolate Satin Pie

1½ cups (12-ounce can) undiluted CARNATION® Evaporated Milk
    2 egg yolks
    2 cups (12-ounce package) NESTLÉ® TOLL HOUSE® Semi-Sweet Chocolate Morsels
    1 prepared 8-inch (6 ounces) chocolate crumb crust
    Whipped cream (optional)
    Chopped nuts (optional)

WHISK together evaporated milk and egg yolks in 2-quart saucepan. Heat over medium-low heat, stirring constantly, until mixture is very hot and thickens slightly; do not boil. Remove from heat; stir in morsels until chocolate is completely melted and mixture is very smooth.

POUR into crust; chill until firm. Top with whipped cream and sprinkle with nuts.
Makes 10 servings

Black Forest Pie

1 tub (8 ounces) COOL WHIP® Whipped Topping, thawed
1 prepared graham cracker crumb crust (6 ounces)
1 cup cold milk
1 package (4-serving size) JELL-O® Chocolate Flavor Instant Pudding &
    Pie Filling
1 cup cherry pie filling

SPREAD 1 cup of the whipped topping onto bottom of crust.

POUR milk into medium bowl. Add pudding mix. Beat with wire whisk 2 minutes. Gently stir in 1½ cups of the whipped topping. Spread pudding mixture over whipped topping in crust.

SPREAD remaining whipped topping over pudding mixture, leaving a 1-inch border and forming a slight depression in center of whipped topping. Spoon cherry pie filling into center.

REFRIGERATE 2 hours or until set.   *Makes 8 servings*

Ice Cream Pudding Pie

Prep Time: *10 minutes*   **Refrigerating Time:** *2 hours*

1 cup cold milk
1 cup ice cream (any flavor), softened
1 package (4-serving size) JELL-O® Instant Pudding & Pie Filling, any
    flavor
1 prepared graham cracker crumb crust (6 ounces)

MIX milk and ice cream in large bowl. Add pudding mix. Beat with electric mixer on lowest speed 1 minute. Pour immediately into crust.

REFRIGERATE 2 hours or until set.   *Makes 8 servings*

Right:
Black Forest Pie

Caramel-Pecan Pie

3 eggs
²⁄₃ cup sugar
1 cup (12-ounce jar) SMUCKER'S® Caramel Topping
¹⁄₄ cup butter or margarine, melted
1 ¹⁄₂ cups pecan halves
1 (9-inch) unbaked pie shell

In mixing bowl, beat eggs slightly with fork. Add sugar; stir until dissolved. Stir in topping and butter; mix well. Stir in pecan halves. Pour filling into pie shell.

Bake at 350°F for 45 minutes or until knife inserted near center comes out clean. Cool thoroughly on rack before serving. Cover, and store in refrigerator.

Makes 6 to 8 servings

Right:
Caramel-Pecan Pie

Above:
*Creamy Chocolate
Pie*

Creamy Chocolate Pie

Prep Time: *10 minutes*   **Refrigerating Time:** *4 hours*

1 ³⁄₄ cups cold milk
2 packages (4-serving size) JELL-O® Chocolate or Chocolate Fudge Flavor Instant Pudding & Pie Filling
1 tub (8 ounces) COOL WHIP® Whipped Topping, thawed
1 prepared chocolate flavor crumb crust (6 ounces)

POUR milk into large bowl. Add pudding mixes. Beat with wire whisk until well mixed. (Mixture will be thick.) Immediately stir in whipped topping. Spoon into crust.

REFRIGERATE 4 hours or until set. Garnish as desired.   *Makes 8 servings*

Summer Lime Pie

1 package (4-serving size) JELL-O® Brand Lime Flavor Gelatin
⅔ cup boiling water
½ teaspoon grated lime peel
3 tablespoons lime juice
½ cup cold water
  Ice cubes
1 tub (8 ounces) COOL WHIP® Whipped Topping, thawed
1 prepared graham cracker crumb crust (6 ounces)
  Lime slices, cut into quarters (optional)

DISSOLVE gelatin completely in boiling water in large bowl. Stir in lime peel and juice. Mix cold water and ice to make 1¼ cups. Add to gelatin, stirring until ice is melted.

STIR in whipped topping with wire whisk until smooth. Refrigerate 10 to 15 minutes or until mixture is very thick and will mound. Spoon into crust.

REFRIGERATE 2 hours or until firm. Garnish with additional whipped topping and lime slices, if desired. Store leftover pie in refrigerator.   *Makes 8 servings*

Luscious Lime Angel Food Cake Rolls

1 package (16 ounces) angel food cake mix
2 drops green food coloring (optional)
2 containers (8 ounces each) lime-flavored nonfat sugar-free yogurt
    Lime slices (optional)

1. Preheat oven to 350°F. Line two 17×11¼×1-inch jelly-roll pans with parchment or waxed paper; set aside.

2. Prepare angel food cake mix according to package directions. Divide batter evenly between prepared pans. Draw knife through batter to remove large air bubbles. Bake 12 minutes or until cakes are lightly browned and toothpick inserted in centers comes out clean.

3. Invert each cake onto separate clean towel. Starting at short end, roll up warm cake, jelly-roll fashion, with towel inside. Cool cakes completely.

4. Place 1 to 2 drops green food coloring in each container of yogurt, if desired; stir well. Unroll cake; remove towel. Spread each cake with 1 container yogurt, leaving 1-inch border. Roll up cake; place seam side down. Slice each cake roll into 8 pieces. Garnish with lime slices, if desired. Serve immediately or refrigerate. *Makes 16 servings*

Below:
*Luscious Lime
Angel Food Cake
Roll*

Angel Almond Cupcakes

1 package DUNCAN HINES® Angel Food Cake Mix
1 ¼ cups water
2 teaspoons almond extract
1 container DUNCAN HINES® Wild Cherry Vanilla Frosting

Preheat oven to 350°F.

Combine cake mix, water and almond extract in large mixing bowl. Beat at low speed with electric mixer until moistened. Beat at medium speed for 1 minute. Line medium muffin pans with paper baking cups. Fill muffin cups two-thirds full. Bake 20 to 25 minutes or until golden brown, cracked and dry. Remove from muffin pans. Cool completely. Frost with frosting. *Makes 30 to 32 cupcakes*

Double Chocolate Cream Cake

1 package DUNCAN HINES® Moist Deluxe Butter Recipe Fudge Cake Mix
1 envelope whipped topping mix
½ cup chocolate syrup
Maraschino cherries with stems for garnish

Preheat oven to 375°F. Grease and flour 13×9-inch pan.

Prepare, bake and cool cake as directed on package.

Prepare whipped topping mix as directed on package. Fold in chocolate syrup until blended. Refrigerate until ready to serve.

To serve, spoon topping over cake slices. Garnish with maraschino cherries.

Makes 12 to 16 servings

Tip: For best consistency, chill chocolate syrup before using.

Right:
*Angel Almond
Cupcakes*

Blueberry Angel Food Cake Rolls

1 package DUNCAN HINES® Angel Food Cake Mix
¼ cup confectioners' sugar, plus additional for dusting
1 (21-ounce) can blueberry pie filling
Mint leaves for garnish (optional)

Preheat oven to 350°F. Line two 15½×10½×1-inch jelly-roll pans with aluminum foil. Prepare cake mix as directed on package. Divide and spread evenly into pans. Cut through batter with knife or spatula to remove large air bubbles. Bake 15 minutes or until set. Invert cakes at once onto clean, lint-free dishtowels dusted with sugar. Remove foil carefully. Roll up each cake with towel jelly-roll fashion, starting at short end. Cool completely.

Unroll cakes. Spread about 1 cup blueberry pie filling to within 1 inch of edge on each cake. Reroll and place, seam side down, on serving plate. Dust with ¼ cup sugar. Garnish with mint leaves, if desired.   *Makes 2 cakes (8 servings each)*

Smart Tip

For a variation in flavor, substitute cherry pie filling for the blueberry pie filling.

Right:
Blueberry Angel Food Cake Roll

Above:
Double Chocolate Snack Cake

Double Chocolate Snack Cake

1 package DUNCAN HINES® Moist Deluxe Devil's Food Cake Mix
1 cup white chocolate chips, divided
½ cup semisweet chocolate chips

Preheat oven to 350°F. Grease and flour 13×9-inch pan.

Prepare cake mix as directed on package. Stir in ½ cup white chocolate chips and semisweet chips. Pour into prepared pan. Bake 35 to 40 minutes or until toothpick inserted in center comes out clean. Remove from oven; sprinkle top with remaining ½ cup white chocolate chips. Serve warm or cool completely in pan.   *Makes 12 to 16 servings*

Apple-Gingerbread Mini Cakes

Prep and Cook Time: *20 minutes*

1 large Cortland or Jonathan apple, cored and quartered
1 package (14½ ounces) gingerbread cake and cookie mix
1 cup water
1 egg
  Powdered sugar

Microwave Directions:

1. Lightly grease 10 (6- to 7-ounce) custard cups; set aside. Grate apple in food processor or with hand-held grater. Combine grated apple, cake mix, water and egg in medium bowl; stir until well blended. Spoon about ⅓ cup mixture into each custard cup, filling cups half full.

2. Arrange 5 cups in microwave oven. Microwave at HIGH 2 minutes. Rotate cups ½ turn. Microwave 1 minute more or until cakes are springy when touched and look slightly moist on top. Cool on wire rack. Repeat with remaining cakes.

3. To unmold cakes, run a small knife around edge of custard cups to loosen cakes while still warm. Invert each cake on cutting board and tap lightly until it drops out. Place each cake on plate. When cool enough, dust with powdered sugar, if desired. Serve warm or at room temperature.   *Makes* 10 *mini cakes*

Serving Tip

For a special touch, serve mini cakes with vanilla ice cream, whipped cream or crème anglaise.

Right:
Apple-Gingerbread Mini Cakes

Below:
Black Forest Torte

Black Forest Torte

1 package DUNCAN HINES® Moist Deluxe Dark Chocolate Fudge Cake
  Mix
2½ cups whipping cream, chilled
2½ tablespoons confectioners' sugar
1 (21-ounce) can cherry pie filling

Preheat oven to 350°F. Grease and flour two 9-inch round cake pans.

Prepare, bake and cool cake as directed on package.

Beat whipping cream in large bowl until soft peaks form. Add sugar gradually. Beat until stiff peaks form.

To assemble, place one cake layer on serving plate. Spread two-thirds cherry pie filling on cake to within ½ inch of edge. Spread 1½ cups whipped cream mixture over cherry pie filling. Top with second cake layer. Frost sides and top with remaining whipped cream mixture. Spread remaining cherry pie filling on top to within 1 inch of edge. Refrigerate until ready to serve.   *Makes 12 to 16 servings*

Tip: Chill the cherry pie filling for easy spreading on cake. Also, garnish the cake with grated semisweet chocolate or white chocolate curls.

Double Berry Layer Cake

1 package DUNCAN HINES® Moist Deluxe® Strawberry Supreme Cake
  Mix
⅔ cup strawberry jam
2½ cups fresh blueberries, rinsed and drained
1 container (8 ounces) frozen whipped topping, thawed
  Fresh strawberry slices, for garnish

1. Preheat oven to 350°F. Grease and flour two 9-inch round cake pans.

2. Prepare, bake and cool cake following package directions for basic recipe.

3. Place one cake layer on serving plate. Spread with ⅓ cup strawberry jam. Arrange 1 cup blueberries on jam. Spread half the whipped topping to within ½ inch of cake edge. Place second cake layer on top. Repeat with remaining ⅓ cup strawberry jam, 1 cup blueberries and remaining whipped topping. Garnish with strawberry slices and remaining ½ cup blueberries. Refrigerate until ready to serve.

Makes 12 servings

Brownie Candy Cups

1 package DUNCAN HINES® Double Fudge Brownie Mix
2 eggs
⅓ cup water
¼ cup vegetable oil
30 miniature peanut butter cup candies

Preheat oven to 350°F. Place 30 (2-inch) foil liners in muffin pans or on cookie sheets.

Combine brownie mix, fudge packet from mix, eggs, water and oil in large bowl. Stir with spoon until well blended, about 50 strokes. Place 2 level tablespoonfuls batter into each foil liner. Bake 10 minutes. Remove from oven. Push 1 peanut butter cup candy in center of each cupcake until even with surface of cupcake. Bake 5 to 7 minutes or until candy is softened. Remove to cooling racks. Cool completely.

Makes 30 brownie cups

Smart Tip

For best results, cut cakes with serrated knife, being sure to clean the knife after each slice.

Below:
Brownie Candy Cups

Dump Cake

1 (20-ounce) can crushed pineapple with juice, undrained
1 (21-ounce) can cherry pie filling
1 package DUNCAN HINES® Moist Deluxe Yellow Cake Mix
1 cup chopped pecans or walnuts
1/2 cup (1 stick) butter or margarine, cut into thin slices

Preheat oven to 350°F. Grease 13×9-inch pan.

Dump pineapple with juice into pan. Spread evenly. Dump in pie filling. Spread evenly. Sprinkle cake mix evenly over cherry layer. Sprinkle pecans over cake mix. Dot with butter. Bake 50 minutes or until top is lightly browned. Serve warm or at room temperature.   *Makes 12 to 16 servings*

Tip: You can use DUNCAN HINES® Moist Deluxe Pineapple Supreme Cake Mix in place of Moist Deluxe Yellow Cake Mix.

Right:
Dump Cake

St. Patrick's Mint Layered Pound Cake

1 frozen loaf pound cake (16 ounces), partially thawed
  Few drops green food color (optional)
1 container (8 ounces) frozen non-dairy whipped topping (3½ cups), thawed
1 HERSHEY'S Cookies 'n' Mint Chocolate Bar (7 ounces), chopped

Slice pound cake horizontally into four layers with serrated knife. Stir green food color into whipped topping, if desired; stir in chocolate bar pieces. Place bottom cake layer on serving plate; spread about 1 cup topping mixture over layer. Repeat layers, ending with topping mixture. Cover; refrigerate. Garnish as desired. Refrigerate leftover cake.   *Makes about 8 to 10 servings*

Above:
St. Patrick's Mint Layered Pound Cake

Fluffy Cheesecake
Prep Time: *15 minutes*

1 package (8 ounces) PHILADELPHIA® Cream Cheese, softened
⅓ cup sugar
1 tub (8 ounces) COOL WHIP® Whipped Topping, thawed
1 prepared graham cracker crumb crust (6 ounces *or* 9 inches)

BEAT cream cheese and sugar in large bowl with wire whisk or electric mixer on high speed until smooth. Gently stir in whipped topping. Spoon into crust.

REFRIGERATE 3 hours or until set. Garnish as desired.   *Makes 8 servings*

Fluffy Cherry Cheesecake: Prepare and refrigerate as directed. Spoon 1½ cups cherry pie filling over top of pie.

Fluffy Cranberry Cheesecake: Beat in 1 cup whole berry cranberry sauce with cream cheese. Proceed as directed.

Fluffy Pumpkin Cheesecake: Increase sugar to ½ cup. Beat in 1 cup canned pumpkin and ½ teaspoon pumpkin pie spice with cream cheese. Proceed as directed.

Fluffy Caramel Pecan Cheesecake: Beat cream cheese and sugar in large bowl with wire whisk until smooth. Gently stir in whipped topping. Spoon 1 cup cream cheese mixture into crust; spread evenly. Top with ⅓ cup KRAFT® Caramel Topping and ¼ cup toasted pecans; spread evenly. Top with remaining cream cheese mixture. Refrigerate 3 hours or until set. Garnish with additional caramel topping, whipped topping and pecans.

Right:
Fluffy Cheesecake

Chocolate Dream Torte

1 package DUNCAN HINES® Moist Deluxe® Dark Chocolate Fudge Cake Mix
1 (6-ounce) package semisweet chocolate chips, melted
1 (8-ounce) container frozen non-dairy whipped topping, thawed, divided
1 container DUNCAN HINES® Milk Chocolate Frosting
3 tablespoons finely chopped dry roasted pistachios

1. Preheat oven to 350°F. Grease and flour two 9-inch round cake pans.

2. Prepare, bake and cool cake as directed on package for basic recipe.

3. For chocolate hearts garnish, spread melted chocolate to ⅛-inch thickness on waxed paper-lined baking sheet. Cut shapes with heart cookie cutter when chocolate begins to set. Refrigerate until firm. Push out heart shapes. Set aside.

4. To assemble, split each cake layer in half horizontally. Place one split cake layer on serving plate. Spread one-third of whipped topping on top. Repeat with remaining layers and whipped topping, leaving top plain. Frost sides and top with frosting. Sprinkle pistachios on top. Position chocolate hearts by pushing points down into cake. Refrigerate until ready to serve.   *Makes 12 to 16 servings*

Chocolate Strawberry Dream Torte: Omit semisweet chocolate chips and chopped pistachios. Proceed as directed through step 2. Fold 1½ cups chopped fresh strawberries into whipped topping in large bowl. Assemble as directed, filling torte with strawberry mixture and frosting with Milk Chocolate Frosting. Garnish cake with strawberry fans and mint leaves, if desired.

Right:
*Chocolate Dream
Torte*

Desserts

Right:
*Easy Citrus Berry
Shortcake (recipe
on page 336)*

Beautiful desserts are always a special addition to a great meal. Cool, fresh sensations are a great way to round out a summer lunch. Or, top a delicately layered treat with warm sauce to finish a tremendous winter supper. Any of these dazzling and easy-to-make delights will have everyone asking for more.

Poached Pears with Raspberry Coulis

Prep Time: 12 *minutes*   **Bake Time:** 25 *minutes*   **Chill Time:** 45 *minutes*

2 firm ripe pears, such as Bosc or Anjou, peeled, halved and cored
1 cup unsweetened white grape juice or sweet wine, such as Rhine or Riesling
1 package (12 ounces) frozen unsweetened raspberries, thawed
1 packet aspartame artificial sweetener *or* equivalent of 2 teaspoons sugar

1. Preheat oven to 350°F. To poach pears, place pears, cut sides down, in shallow ovenproof baking dish large enough to hold pears in one layer. Pour grape juice over pears. Bake 25 to 30 minutes or until pears are tender when pierced with sharp knife, basting with juices in dish every 10 minutes. Let pears stand in juices until cooled to room temperature, occasionally spooning juices over pears. (Pears may be served at room temperature or covered and chilled up to 3 hours before serving.)

2. To prepare coulis, purée thawed raspberries with their juices in food processor or blender. Strain out and discard seeds, pushing firmly on solids to extract juices. Stir in sweetener. Arrange pears on serving plates; top with coulis. Or, spoon coulis onto serving plates and top with pears.   *Makes* 4 *servings*

Right:
Poached Pears with
Raspberry Coulis

Brownie Berry Parfaits
Prep Time: 10 *minutes*

1 box (10 ounces) BIRDS EYE® frozen Raspberries*
4 large prepared brownies, cut into cubes
1 pint vanilla or chocolate ice cream
4 tablespoons chocolate syrup
2 tablespoons chopped walnuts

Or, substitute Birds Eye® frozen Strawberries.

• Thaw raspberries according to package directions.

• Divide half the brownie cubes among four parfait glasses. Top with half the ice cream and raspberries. Repeat layers with remaining brownie cubes, ice cream and raspberries.

• Drizzle chocolate syrup over each dessert; sprinkle with walnuts.

Makes 4 servings

Berried Cantaloupe with Honey Dressing

1 cup plain yogurt
2 tablespoons honey
2 teaspoons grated orange peel
2 small cantaloupes
2 cups raspberries

1. Combine yogurt, honey and orange peel; cover. Refrigerate.

2. Cut cantaloupes in half; remove seeds. Cover; refrigerate.

3. When ready to serve, place cantaloupe halves in individual bowls; fill centers with raspberries. Drizzle with dressing.

Makes 4 servings

Serving Tip

Most chocolate or fruit sauces can be served warm or cold over ice cream. Make them several days ahead, then store, tightly covered, in refrigerator.

Right:
Brownie Berry Parfaits

Mimosa Mold

Prep Time: 15 *minutes*   **Refrigerating Time:** 4¾ *hours*

1½ cups boiling water
1 package (8-serving size) *or* 2 packages (4-serving size) JELL-O® Brand
      Sparkling White Grape or Lemon Flavor Gelatin Dessert
2 cups cold seltzer or club soda
1 can (11 ounces) mandarin orange segments, drained
1 cup sliced strawberries

STIR boiling water into gelatin in large bowl at least 2 minutes or until completely dissolved. Refrigerate 15 minutes. Gently stir in seltzer. Refrigerate about 30 minutes or until slightly thickened (consistency of unbeaten egg whites). Gently stir about 15 seconds. Stir in oranges and strawberries. Pour into 6-cup mold.

REFRIGERATE 4 hours or until firm. Unmold.* Garnish as desired. Store leftover gelatin mold in refrigerator.   *Makes 12 servings*

****Unmolding**: Dip mold in warm water for about 15 seconds. Gently pull gelatin from around edges with moist fingers. Place moistened serving plate on top of mold. Invert mold and plate; holding mold and plate together, shake slightly to loosen. Gently remove mold and center gelatin on plate.*

Right:
Mimosa Mold

Above:
*Luscious Chocolate
Covered
Strawberries*

Luscious Chocolate Covered Strawberries

3 squares (1 ounce each) semi-sweet chocolate
2 tablespoons I CAN'T BELIEVE IT'S NOT BUTTER!® Spread
1 tablespoon coffee liqueur (optional)
6 to 8 large strawberries with stems

Microwave Directions: In small microwave-safe bowl, microwave chocolate and I Can't Believe It's Not Butter! Spread at HIGH (Full Power) 1 minute or until chocolate is melted; stir until smooth. Stir in liqueur. Dip strawberries in chocolate mixture, then refrigerate on waxed paper-lined baking sheet until chocolate is set, at least 1 hour.   *Makes 6 to 8 strawberries*

Chocolate Plunge

Prep Time: 10 *minutes*

²/₃ **cup KARO® Light or Dark Corn Syrup**
¹/₂ **cup heavy cream**
 8 **squares (1 ounce each) semisweet chocolate**
   Assorted fresh fruit

1. In medium saucepan combine corn syrup and cream. Bring to a boil over medium heat. Remove from heat.

2. Add chocolate; stir until completely melted.

3. Serve warm as a dip for fruit.   *Makes 1 ½ cups*

Try some of these "dippers": Candied pineapple, dried apricots, waffle squares, ladyfingers, cubed pound cake, macaroons, pretzels, croissants, mint cookies or peanut butter cookies.

Chocolate Plunge can be made a day ahead. Store covered in refrigerator. Reheat before serving.

Microwave Plunge: In medium microwavable bowl, combine corn syrup and cream. Microwave at HIGH 1 ½ minutes or until boiling. Add chocolate; stir until completely melted. Serve as directed.

Quick Tip

Check out the cut-up fresh fruit in your supermarket salad bar for a no-fuss way to "prepare" fruit for last-minute desserts. Add a festive touch with a variety of colors, shapes and textures.

Right:
Chocolate Plunge

Watermelon Ice

4 cups seeded 1-inch watermelon chunks
¼ cup thawed frozen unsweetened pineapple juice concentrate
2 tablespoons fresh lime juice
　Fresh melon balls (optional)
　Fresh mint leaves (optional)

Place melon chunks in single layer in plastic freezer bag; freeze until firm, about 8 hours. Place frozen melon in food processor container fitted with steel blade. Let stand 15 minutes to soften slightly. Add pineapple juice and lime juice. Remove plunger from top of food processor to allow air to be incorporated. Process until smooth, scraping down sides of container frequently. Spoon into individual dessert dishes. Garnish with melon balls and mint leaves, if desired. Freeze leftovers. *Makes 6 servings*

Honeydew Ice: Substitute honeydew for watermelon and unsweetened pineapple-guava-orange juice concentrate for pineapple juice concentrate.

Cantaloupe Ice: Substitute cantaloupe for watermelon and unsweetened pineapple-guava-orange juice concentrate for pineapple juice concentrate.

Smart Tip

Fruit ice may be transferred to an airtight container and frozen up to 1 month. Let stand at room temperature 10 minutes to soften slightly before serving.

Right (clockwise from top):
Honey Ice, Cantalope Ice and Watermelon Ice

Festive Stuffed Dates
Prep Time: *25 minutes*

1 box (8 ounces) DOLE® Whole Pitted Dates
1 package (3 ounces) reduced fat cream cheese, softened
¼ cup powdered sugar
1 tablespoon grated peel of 1 DOLE® Orange

• Make slit in center of each date. Combine cream cheese, powdered sugar and orange peel. Fill centers of dates with cream cheese mixture. Refrigerate.

• Dust with additional powdered sugar just before serving, if desired.
Makes about 27 stuffed dates

Above:
Take-Along Cake

Smart Tip

To keep leftover pecans fresh, store them in the freezer in an airtight container.

Take-Along Cake

1 package DUNCAN HINES® Moist Deluxe® Swiss Chocolate Cake Mix
1 (12-ounce) package semisweet chocolate chips
1 cup miniature marshmallows
¼ cup butter or margarine, melted
½ cup packed brown sugar
½ cup chopped pecans or walnuts

Preheat oven to 350°F. Grease and flour 13×9-inch pan.

Prepare cake mix as directed on package. Add chips and marshmallows to batter. Pour into prepared pan. Drizzle melted butter over batter. Sprinkle with sugar and top with pecans. Bake 45 to 55 minutes or until toothpick inserted in center comes out clean. Serve warm or cool completely in pan.   *Makes 12 to 16 servings*

Easy Citrus Berry Shortcake

1 individual sponge cake
1 tablespoon orange juice
¼ cup lemon chiffon sugar-free, nonfat yogurt
¼ cup thawed frozen fat-free nondairy whipped topping
⅔ cup sliced strawberries or raspberries
Mint leaves (optional)

1. Place individual sponge cake on serving plate. Drizzle with orange juice.

2. Fold together yogurt and whipped topping. Spoon half of mixture onto cake. Top with berries and remaining yogurt mixture. Garnish with mint leaves, if desired.

Makes 1 serving

Fruit Freezies

1 ½ cups (12 ounces) canned or thawed frozen peach slices, drained
¾ cup peach nectar
1 tablespoon sugar
¼ to ½ teaspoon coconut extract (optional)

1. Place peaches, nectar, sugar and extract, if desired, in food processor or blender container; process until smooth.

2. Spoon 2 tablespoons fruit mixture into each section of ice cube trays.*

3. Freeze until almost firm. Insert frill pick into each cube; freeze until firm.

Makes 12 servings

Or, pour ⅓ cup fruit mixture into each of 8 plastic pop molds or small paper or plastic cups. Freeze until almost firm. Insert wooden stick into each mold; freeze until firm. Makes 8 servings.

Apricot Freezies: Substitute canned apricot halves for peach slices and apricot nectar for peach nectar.

Pear Freezies: Substitute canned pear slices for peach slices, pear nectar for peach nectar and almond extract for coconut extract.

Pineapple Freezies: Substitute crushed pineapple for peach slices and unsweetened pineapple juice for peach nectar.

Mango Freezies: Substitute chopped fresh mango for canned peach slices and mango nectar for peach nectar. Omit coconut extract.

Below:
Fruit Freezies

Banana Cream Parfaits

Prep and Cook Time: 25 *minutes*   **Chill Time:** *at least 1 hour*

   1 package (4 serving size) sugar-free vanilla pudding and pie filling mix
   2 cups low-fat 1% milk
   1 cup coarsely crushed sugar-free cookies
   2 large ripe bananas, peeled and sliced
      Mint sprigs (optional)

1. Prepare pudding according to package directions, using low-fat milk; cool 10 minutes, stirring occasionally.

2. In parfait or wine glasses, layer 2 tablespoons cookie crumbs, ¼ cup banana slices and ¼ cup pudding. Repeat layering. Cover; chill at least 1 hour or up to 6 hours before serving. Garnish with mint sprigs, if desired.   *Makes 4 servings*

Variation: Sugar-free chocolate pudding and pie filling mix may be substituted for vanilla pudding.

Right:
*Banana Cream
Parfaits*

Strawberry Miracle Mold

Prep Time: 10 *minutes plus refrigerating*

1 ½ cups boiling water
   2 packages (4-serving size) JELL-O® Brand Strawberry Flavor Gelatin
1 ¾ cups cold water
   ½ cup MIRACLE WHIP® Salad Dressing
      Assorted fruit

Stir boiling water into gelatin in medium bowl 2 minutes or until dissolved. Stir in cold water. Gradually whisk gelatin into salad dressing in large bowl until well blended.

Pour into 1-quart mold or glass serving bowl that has been lightly sprayed with nonstick cooking spray. Refrigerate until firm. Unmold onto serving plate; serve with fruit.   *Makes 4 to 6 servings*

Above:
*Strawberry Miracle
Mold*

White Chocolate Strawberry Mousse with Raspberries

1 (3-ounce) package ROYAL® Strawberry Gelatin
2 tablespoons water
4 ounces white chocolate, broken into chunks
2 cups heavy cream, whipped
    Raspberries and mint sprigs, optional

1. Heat gelatin and water in double boiler over medium heat until gelatin dissolves and mixture is very syrupy, stirring occasionally. Add chocolate; cook until smooth, stirring constantly. Remove from heat. Fold in whipped cream.

2. Spread mixture into 9×5×3-inch loaf pan. Chill until set, about 2 hours.

3. Scoop mixture into 8 dessert dishes. Garnish with raspberries and mint if desired. *Makes 8 (⅓-cup) servings*

Right:
White Chocolate Strawberry Mousse with Raspberries

Above:
Grilled Banana Splits

Grilled Banana Splits

2 large ripe firm bananas
1 teaspoon melted butter
4 tablespoons reduced-sugar, reduced-calorie, fat-free chocolate syrup
1 teaspoon orange liqueur (optional)
1 ⅓ cups sugar-free vanilla ice cream
¼ cup toasted sliced almonds

1. Prepare grill for direct cooking. Cut unpeeled bananas lengthwise; brush melted butter over cut sides. Grill bananas, cut sides down, over medium-hot coals 2 minutes or until lightly browned; turn. Grill 2 minutes or until tender.

2. Combine syrup and liqueur, if desired, in small bowl. Cut bananas in half crosswise; carefully remove peel. Place 2 pieces banana in each bowl; top with ⅓ cup ice cream, 1 tablespoon chocolate syrup and ¼ of nuts; serve immediately. *Makes 4 servings*

**Right
(clockwise
from top):**
*Caramel-Nut
Apple, Caramel-
Chocolate Apple
and Caramel-
Marshmallow
Apple*

Cheesecake Creme Dip

Prep Time: *5 minutes plus refrigerating*

**1 package (8 ounces) PHILADELPHIA® Cream Cheese, softened
1 jar (7 ounces) marshmallow creme**

MIX cream cheese and marshmallow creme with electric mixer on medium speed until well blended. Refrigerate.

SERVE with assorted cut-up fresh fruit or pound cake cubes. Garnish as desired.

Makes 1¾ cups

Caramel-Marshmallow Apples

**1 package (14 ounces) caramels
1 cup miniature marshmallows
1 tablespoon water
5 or 6 small apples**

1. Line baking sheet with buttered waxed paper; set aside.

2. Combine caramels, marshmallows and water in medium saucepan. Cook over medium heat, stirring constantly, until caramels melt. Cool slightly while preparing apples.

3. Rinse and thoroughly dry apples. Insert flat sticks in stem ends of apples.

4. Dip each apple in caramel mixture, coating apples. Remove excess caramel mixture by scraping apple bottoms across rim of saucepan. Place on prepared baking sheet. Refrigerate until firm.   *Makes 5 or 6 apples*

Caramel-Nut Apples: Roll coated apples in chopped nuts before refrigerating.

Caramel-Chocolate Apples: Drizzle melted milk chocolate over coated apples before refrigerating.

Englishman's Trifle

Prep Time: *20 minutes*

1 box (10 ounces) BIRDS EYE® frozen Strawberries*
1 package (3.4 ounces) vanilla instant pudding
1½ cups milk
1 cup thawed frozen whipped topping
8 thin slices fresh or thawed frozen pound cake
½ cup toasted sliced almonds
¼ cup mini semisweet chocolate chips (optional)

Or, substitute Birds Eye® frozen Raspberries.

• Thaw strawberries according to package directions.

• Prepare pudding with 1½ cups milk according to package directions. Let stand 5 minutes; gently stir in whipped topping.

• Place 1 slice cake in each of 4 individual serving bowls. Spoon half the strawberries over cake. Top with half the pudding mixture, almonds and chocolate chips.

• Repeat layers of cake, strawberries, pudding, almonds and chips. Cover and chill until ready to serve.

Makes 4 servings

Right:
Englishman's Trifle

Brownie Baked Alaskas

2 purchased brownies (2½ inches square)
2 scoops fudge swirl ice cream (or favorite flavor)
⅓ cup semisweet chocolate chips
2 tablespoons light corn syrup or milk
2 egg whites
¼ cup sugar

1. Preheat oven to 500°F. Place brownies on small cookie sheet; top each with scoop of ice cream and place in freezer.

2. Melt chocolate chips in small saucepan over low heat. Stir in corn syrup; set aside and keep warm.

3. Beat egg whites to soft peaks in small bowl. Gradually beat in sugar; continue beating until stiff peaks form. Spread egg white mixture over ice cream and brownies with small spatula. (Ice cream and brownies should be completely covered with egg white mixture.)

4. Bake 2 to 3 minutes or until meringue is golden. Spread chocolate sauce on serving plates; place baked Alaskas over sauce. *Makes 2 servings*

Cool Cappuccino Shake
Prep time: *5 minutes*

1 cup milk
1 envelope MAXWELL HOUSE® Cappuccino, any flavor
½ cup COOL WHIP® Whipped Topping, frozen

PLACE milk and cappuccino in blender container; cover. Blend on high speed until cappuccino is dissolved. Add whipped topping; cover. Blend until smooth. Serve at once with additional whipped topping, if desired. Garnish as desired.

Makes 1 serving

Right:
*Brownie Baked
Alaskas*

Cookies

Cookies are easily any child's favorite...and there's a child hidden in every adult. Bring a smile to everyone's face with these uncomplicated treats the kids can help you create. Whip up a bunch of crunchy crescents or blissful bar cookies; you'll come away a winner and they'll leave with a handful of happiness.

Right:
Chocolate Macadamia Cookies (recipe on page 350)

Derby Brownies

1 package DUNCAN HINES® Walnut Brownie Mix
½ cup (1 stick) butter or margarine, softened
1 pound confectioners' sugar (about 3½ to 4 cups)
2 tablespoons bourbon or milk
1 container DUNCAN HINES® Dark Chocolate Frosting

Preheat oven to 350°F. Grease bottom only of 13×9-inch pan.

Prepare brownie mix as directed on package for cake-like brownies. Pour into prepared pan. Bake 24 to 27 minutes or until set. Cool completely in pan. Beat butter until smooth in large mixing bowl; stir in sugar and bourbon. Beat until smooth and of spreading consistency. Spread over brownies; chill. Top with frosting. Chill 2 to 4 hours. Cut into bars and serve at room temperature.

Makes 24 brownies

Chocolate Macadamia Cookies

1 package DUNCAN HINES® Chocolate Chip Cookie Mix
¼ cup unsweetened cocoa powder
⅓ cup vegetable oil
1 egg
3 tablespoons water
⅔ cup coarsely chopped macadamia nuts

Preheat oven to 375°F.

Combine cookie mix and cocoa in large bowl. Add oil, egg and water. Stir until thoroughly blended. Stir in macadamia nuts. Drop by rounded teaspoonfuls 2 inches apart onto *ungreased* cookie sheets.

Bake 8 to 10 minutes or until set. Cool 1 minute on cookie sheets. Remove to cooling racks. Cool completely.

Makes 3 dozen cookies

Right:
Derby Brownies

Cherry Surprises

1 package DUNCAN HINES® Golden Sugar Cookie Mix
36 to 42 candied cherries
$\frac{1}{2}$ cup semisweet chocolate chips
1 teaspoon shortening

Preheat oven to 375°F. Grease cookie sheets.

Prepare cookie mix as directed on package. Shape thin layer of dough around each cherry. Place 2 inches apart on prepared cookie sheets. Bake 8 minutes or until set but not browned. Cool 1 minute on cookie sheets. Remove to cooling racks. Cool completely.

Combine chips and shortening in small resealable plastic bag. Place bag in bowl of hot water for several minutes. Dry bag with towel. Knead until blended and chocolate is smooth. Snip pinpoint hole in corner of bag. Drizzle chocolate over cookies. Allow drizzle to set before storing between layers of waxed paper in airtight container.   *Makes 3 to 3½ dozen cookies*

Smart Tip

Well-drained maraschino cherries may be substituted for candied cherries.

Easy Mint Brownies

1 package DUNCAN HINES® Chocolate Lovers Walnut Brownie Mix
4 bars (5.3 ounces each) cookies and mint chocolate candy bars
$\frac{1}{3}$ cup chopped walnuts, for garnish (optional)

1. Preheat oven to 350°F. Grease bottom of 13×9×2-inch pan.

2. Prepare and bake brownies, following package directions for basic recipe chewy brownies. Break chocolate candy bars along scored lines. Place pieces immediately on hot brownies. Cover pan with aluminum foil for 3 to 5 minutes or until chocolate is shiny and soft. Spread gently to cover surface of brownies. Sprinkle with chopped walnuts, if desired. Cool completely. Cut into bars.   *Makes 18 brownies*

Right:
Cherry Surprises

Chocolate Spritz Cookies

1 package DUNCAN HINES® Golden Sugar Cookie Mix
⅓ cup unsweetened cocoa powder
1 egg
⅓ cup vegetable oil
2 tablespoons water

1. Preheat oven to 375°F.

2. Combine cookie mix and cocoa in large mixing bowl. Stir until blended. Add egg, oil and water. Stir until thoroughly blended.

3. Fill cookie press with dough. Press desired shapes 2 inches apart onto ungreased cookie sheets. Bake at 375°F for 6 to 8 minutes or until set. Cool 1 minute on baking sheets. Remove to cooling racks. Cool completely.

Makes 5 to 6 dozen cookies

Note: For a tasty no-cholesterol variation, substitute 2 egg whites for whole egg.

Chocolate Fudge-Peanut Butter Balls

2 cups (11½ ounces) milk chocolate chips
¼ cup half-and-half
⅓ cup creamy peanut butter
⅓ cup chopped peanuts

1. Melt chips with half-and-half in heavy medium saucepan over low heat, stirring occasionally. Whisk in peanut butter until blended. Refrigerate until mixture is firm enough to shape into balls, but still soft, about 30 minutes, stirring occasionally.

2. Spread peanuts on waxed paper.

3. Shape scant 1 tablespoonful of the mixture into 1-inch balls. Roll balls in peanuts. Store in refrigerator.

Makes about 32 balls

Right:
Chocolate Spritz
Cookies

Chocolate Peanut Butter Cookies

    1 package DUNCAN HINES® Moist Deluxe Devil's Food Cake Mix
    ¾ cup crunchy peanut butter
    2 eggs
    2 tablespoons milk
    1 cup candy-coated peanut butter pieces

Preheat oven to 350°F. Grease cookie sheets.

Combine cake mix, peanut butter, eggs and milk in large mixing bowl. Beat at low speed with electric mixer until blended. Stir in peanut butter pieces.

Drop dough by slightly rounded tablespoonfuls onto prepared cookie sheets. Bake 7 to 9 minutes or until lightly browned. Cool 2 minutes on cookie sheets. Remove to cooling racks. *Makes about 3½ dozen cookies*

Smart Tip

You can use 1 cup peanut butter chips in place of peanut butter pieces.

Banana Rum Brownies
Prep Time: 15 *minutes*   **Bake Time:** 40 *minutes*

    1 box (about 21 ounces) brownie mix
    ¼ cup chocolate milk or regular milk
    1 tablespoon rum extract
    3 DOLE® Bananas, cubed
    ½ cup toasted chopped pecans

• Prepare brownie mix as directed on package in large bowl; set aside.

• Heat milk and extract in medium saucepan, until hot. Add bananas and stir for 1 minute to heat through.

• Pour banana mixture and nuts into brownie mix and stir. Pour into lightly greased 9-inch square pan.

• Bake at 350°F, 35 to 40 minutes or until toothpick inserted in center comes out clean. Sprinkle with powdered sugar, if desired. Cut into bars. *Makes 16 servings*

Right:
Chocolate Peanut Butter Cookies

Chocolate Chip Raspberry Jumbles

1 package DUNCAN HINES® Chocolate Chip Cookie Mix
½ cup seedless red raspberry jam

Preheat oven to 350°F.

Prepare chocolate chip cookie mix as directed on package. Reserve ½ cup dough.

Spread remaining dough into *ungreased* 9-inch square pan. Spread jam over base. Drop reserved dough by measuring teaspoonfuls randomly over jam. Bake 20 to 25 minutes or until golden brown. Cool completely. Cut into bars.

Makes 16 bars

The Original Rice Krispies Treats® Recipe

3 tablespoons margarine
1 package (10 ounces, about 40) regular marshmallows *or* 4 cups
    miniature marshmallows
6 cups KELLOGG'S® RICE KRISPIES® cereal
Vegetable cooking spray

1. Melt margarine in large saucepan over low heat. Add marshmallows and stir until completely melted. Remove from heat.

2. Add Kellogg's Rice Krispies® cereal. Stir until well coated.

3. Using buttered spatula or waxed paper, press mixture evenly into 13×9×2-inch pan coated with cooking spray. Cut into 2×2-inch squares when cool.

Makes 24 (2-inch-square) treats

Note: Use fresh marshmallows for best results.

Microwave Directions: Microwave margarine and marshmallows at HIGH 2 minutes in microwave-safe mixing bowl. Stir to combine. Microwave at HIGH 1 minute longer. Stir until smooth. Add cereal. Stir until well coated. Press into pan as directed in Step 3.

Right:
Chocolate Chip
Raspberry Jumbles

Butterscotch Crescents

¹/₂ cup HERSHEY¿S Butterscotch Chips
¹/₄ cup MOUNDS® Sweetened Coconut Flakes
2 tablespoons finely chopped nuts
1 can (8 ounces) refrigerated quick crescent dinner rolls
Powdered sugar

1. Heat oven to 375°F. Stir together butterscotch chips, coconut and nuts in small bowl. Unroll crescent roll dough to form eight triangles. Lightly sprinkle 1 heaping tablespoon butterscotch mixture on top of each; gently press into dough. Starting at short side of each triangle, roll dough to opposite point. Place rolls, point side down, on ungreased cookie sheet; curve into crescent shapes.

2. Bake 10 to 12 minutes or until golden brown. Sprinkle with powdered sugar. Serve warm.

Makes 8 crescents

Brown Sugar Shortbread

1 cup (2 sticks) I CAN'T BELIEVE IT'S NOT BUTTER!® Spread
³/₄ cup firmly packed light brown sugar
2 cups all-purpose flour
¹/₃ cup semisweet chocolate chips, melted

Preheat oven to 325°F. Grease 9-inch round cake pan; set aside.

In large bowl, with electric mixer, beat I Can't Believe It's Not Butter! Spread and brown sugar until light and fluffy, about 5 minutes. Gradually add flour and beat on low until blended. Spread mixture into prepared pan and press into even layer. With knife, score surface into 8 pie-shaped wedges.

Bake 30 minutes or until lightly golden. On wire rack, cool 20 minutes; remove from pan and cool completely. To serve, pour melted chocolate into small plastic storage bag. Snip corner and drizzle chocolate over shortbread. Cut into wedges.

Makes 8 servings

Tony's Tiger Bites™

   1 package (10 ounces) regular-size marshmallows (about 40)
   ¼ cup margarine
   ⅓ cup peanut butter
7½ cups KELLOGG'S® FROSTED FLAKES® cereal

Microwave Directions:

1. In 4-quart microwave-safe bowl, melt marshmallows and margarine at HIGH 3 minutes or until melted, stirring after 1½ minutes.

2. Stir in peanut butter until mixture is smooth. Add KELLOGG'S FROSTED FLAKES® cereal, stirring until well coated.

3. Using buttered spatula or waxed paper, press mixture into 13×9×2 inch pan coated with cooking spray. Cut into 1½×2-inch bars when cool.   *Makes 32 bars*

Note: Use fresh marshmallows for best results.

Range-Top Directions: Melt margarine in large saucepan over low heat. Add marshmallows, stirring until completely melted. Remove from heat. Follow steps 2 and 3 above.

Polka Dot Macaroons

   1 14-ounce bag (5 cups) shredded coconut
   1 14-ounce can sweetened condensed milk
   ½ cup all-purpose flour
1¾ cups "M&M's"® Chocolate Mini Baking Bits

Preheat oven to 350°F. Grease cookie sheets; set aside. In large bowl, combine coconut, condensed milk and flour until well blended. Stir in "M&M's"® Chocolate Mini Baking Bits. Drop by rounded tablespoonfuls about 2 inches apart onto prepared cookie sheets. Bake 8 to 10 minutes or until edges are golden. Cool completely on wire racks. Store in tightly covered container.

Makes about 5 dozen cookies

Above:
*Polka Dot
Macaroons*

Nutty Lemon Crescents

1 package (18 ounces) refrigerated sugar cookie dough
1 cup chopped pecans, toasted
1 tablespoon grated lemon peel
1 1/2 cups powdered sugar, divided

1. Preheat oven to 375°F. Remove dough from wrapper according to package directions.

2. Combine dough, pecans and lemon peel in large bowl. Stir until thoroughly blended. Shape level tablespoonfuls of dough into crescent shapes. Place 2 inches apart on ungreased cookie sheets. Bake 8 to 9 minutes or until set and very lightly browned. Cool 2 minutes on cookie sheets. Remove to wire racks.

3. Place 1 cup powdered sugar in shallow bowl. Roll warm cookies in powdered sugar. Cool completely. Sift remaining 1/2 cup powdered sugar over cookies just before serving. *Makes about 4 dozen cookies*

Butter Fudge Fingers

1 package DUNCAN HINES® Chocolate Lovers Chewy Fudge Brownie Mix
1 container DUNCAN HINES® Buttercream Frosting
1/4 cup semi-sweet chocolate chips
1 1/2 teaspoons shortening plus additional for greasing

1. Preheat oven to 350°F. Grease bottom of 13×9×2-inch pan.

2. Prepare, bake and cool brownies following package directions for basic recipe chewy brownies. Spread with Buttercream frosting.

3. Place chocolate chips and shortening in small resealable plastic bag; seal. Microwave at HIGH (100% power) 30 seconds, adding 15 to 30 seconds more if needed. Knead until blended. Snip pinpoint hole in corner of bag. Drizzle chocolate over frosting. Allow chocolate to set before cutting into bars.

Makes 18 brownies

Smart Tip

Another method for melting the chocolate and shortening in the sealed bag is to place the bag in a bowl of hot water for several minutes. Dry bag with paper towel. Knead, snip and pipe as directed.

Right:
Nutty Lemon Crescents

Double Chocolate Chewies

1 package DUNCAN HINES® Moist Deluxe Butter Recipe Fudge Cake Mix
2 eggs
½ cup butter or margarine, melted
1 package (6 ounces) semi-sweet chocolate chips
1 cup chopped nuts
Confectioners' sugar (optional)

1. Preheat oven to 350°F. Grease 13×9×2-inch pan.

2. Combine cake mix, eggs and melted butter in large bowl. Stir until thoroughly blended. (Mixture will be stiff.) Stir in chocolate chips and nuts. Press mixture evenly in greased pan. Bake 25 to 30 minutes or until toothpick inserted in center comes out clean. *Do not overbake.* Cool completely. Cut into bars. Dust with confectioners' sugar, if desired.   *Makes 36 bars*

Crispy Cocoa Bars

¼ cup (½ stick) margarine
¼ cup HERSHEY'S Cocoa
5 cups miniature marshmallows
5 cups crisp rice cereal

1. Spray 13×9×2-inch pan with vegetable cooking spray.

2. Melt margarine in large saucepan over low heat; stir in cocoa and marshmallows. Cook over low heat, stirring constantly, until marshmallows are melted and mixture is smooth and well blended. Continue cooking 1 minute, stirring constantly. Remove from heat.

3. Add cereal; stir until coated. Lightly spray spatula with vegetable cooking spray; press mixture into prepared pan. Cool completely. Cut into bars.
Makes 24 bars

Smart Tip

For a special effect, cut a paper towel into ¼-inch-wide strips. Place strips in diagonal pattern on top of cooled bars before cutting. Place confectioners' sugar in tea strainer. Tap strainer lightly to dust surface with sugar. Carefully remove strips.

Right:
Double Chocolate Chewies

Dark Chocolate Truffles

1²/₃ cups chopped semisweet chocolate or semisweet chocolate chips
6 tablespoons whipping cream*
1 tablespoon cold butter or margarine, cut into pieces
1 teaspoon vanilla
¹/₂ cup chopped macadamia nuts or toffee, or chocolate decors

*To flavor with liqueur, reduce cream to ¹/₄ cup. Stir 2 tablespoons liqueur into chocolate mixture along with vanilla.

1. Place chocolate in small bowl. Combine whipping cream and butter in small saucepan. Simmer over medium-high heat until butter melts, stirring constantly. Pour over chocolate; stir once.

2. Cover bowl; let stand 3 to 5 minutes. Uncover; stir until chocolate is melted and mixture is smooth. Stir in vanilla and liqueur, if using. Cover. Refrigerate 15 minutes or until mixture is firm enough to hold its shape.

3. Place level tablespoonfuls mixture on plate. Cover; refrigerate 2 hours or until fudgy, but not soft.

4. Place nuts in medium bowl. Roll each tablespoon chocolate mixture into ball. Roll in nuts to evenly coat. (Warm hands and room temperature quickly soften chocolate, making it difficult to form balls. Keeping chocolate chilled prevents sticking.)

5. Store tightly covered in refrigerator up to 3 weeks. Serve chilled or let stand at room temperature 15 to 20 minutes before serving.   *Makes 18 truffles*

Right:
Dark Chocolate Truffles, Gianduia Truffles (page 368) and White Chocolate Truffles (page 373)

Gianduia Truffles

6 tablespoons butter or margarine*
6 ounces (1 cup) chopped milk chocolate or milk chocolate chips
1 cup toasted hazelnuts or unblanched almonds
½ cup chopped macadamia nuts or toffee, or chocolate decors

To flavor with liqueur, reduce butter to 2 tablespoons. Stir 2 tablespoons hazelnut- or almond-flavored liqueur into melted chocolate mixture.

1. Melt butter in small saucepan over low heat, stirring occasionally with wooden spoon. Remove saucepan from heat. Add chocolate; stir until melted. Stir in hazelnuts. Refrigerate 15 minutes or until firm enough to hold its shape.

2. Place level tablespoonfuls mixture on plate. Cover; refrigerate 2 hours or until fudgy, but not soft.

3. Place chopped macadamia nuts in medium bowl. Roll each tablespoon chocolate mixture into ball. Roll in chopped nuts to evenly coat. (Warm hands and room temperature quickly soften chocolate, making it difficult to form balls. Keeping chocolate chilled prevents sticking.)

4. Store tightly covered in refrigerator up to 3 weeks. Serve chilled or let stand at room temperature 15 to 20 minutes before serving. *Makes 18 truffles*

Strawberry Hearts

1 roll (17 to 18 ounces) refrigerated sugar cookie dough
2 packages (8 ounces *each*) cream cheese, softened
²/₃ cup powdered sugar
1 teaspoon vanilla extract
2 cups sliced fresh strawberries

Roll out dough, cut out hearts and bake as directed on package.

Combine cream cheese, sugar and vanilla; mix well.

Spread evenly onto cooled hearts; top evenly with strawberries.

Makes about 2 dozen hearts

Above:
Strawberry Hearts

Chewy Fudge Brownies

1 package DUNCAN HINES® Chocolate Lovers Chewy Fudge Brownie Mix
1 egg
2 tablespoons water
¹/₃ cup unsweetened apple sauce

1. Preheat oven to 350°F. Lightly grease 13×9-inch pan.

2. Follow instructions on box for PREPARE and MAKE BATTER. Spread batter in pan. Bake at 350°F 23 to 26 minutes or until set. Cool completely.

Makes 20 brownies

Tip: If using a 9×9-inch pan, bake brownies 33 to 36 minutes; if using an 8×8-inch pan, bake brownies 34 to 37 minutes.

S'more Snack Treats

Prep and Cook Time: 15 *minutes*   **Chill Time:** 20 *minutes*

44 HONEY MAID® Honey Graham squares (2 sleeves)
3 tablespoons margarine or butter
1 (10-ounce) package marshmallows
¾ cup miniature semisweet chocolate chips

1. Break grahams into bite-size pieces; set aside.

2. Heat margarine or butter in large saucepan over medium heat until melted. Add marshmallows, stirring constantly until melted.

3. Stir broken crackers into marshmallow mixture to coat evenly. Spread mixture into lightly greased 13×9×2-inch pan; sprinkle with chocolate chips, pressing chips lightly with greased hands.

4. Refrigerate at least 20 minutes before cutting into squares.   *Makes 12 s'mores*

Scottish Shortbread

5 cups all-purpose flour
1 cup rice flour
2 cups butter, softened
1 cup sugar
Candied fruit (optional)

Preheat oven to 325°F. Sift together flours. Beat butter and sugar in large bowl with electric mixer until creamy. Blend in ¾ of flour until mixture resembles fine crumbs. Stir in remaining flour by hand. Press dough firmly into ungreased 15½×10½×1-inch jelly-roll pan or two 9-inch fluted tart pans; crimp and flute edges of dough in jelly-roll pan, if desired. Bake 40 to 45 minutes or until light brown. Place pan on wire rack. Cut into bars or wedges while warm. Decorate with candied fruit, if desired. Cool completely. Store in airtight containers.

Makes about 4 dozen bars or 24 wedges

Quick Tip

Soften butter for easier spreading or for use in batters and doughs. Place 1 stick of butter on a microwavable plate and heat at LOW (30% power) about 30 seconds or just until softened.

Right:
S'more Snack Treats

Peanut Maple Triangles

Prep and Bake Time: 30 *minutes*

1 ¼ cups powdered sugar, divided
½ cup creamy peanut butter
¼ cup plus 3 tablespoons maple-flavored syrup, divided
1 package (17½ ounces) frozen puff pastry dough, thawed
1 to 2 tablespoons water

1. Preheat oven to 400°F. Combine ¼ cup powdered sugar, peanut butter and ¼ cup maple syrup in small bowl until well blended; set aside.

2. Cut pastry dough into 3-inch-wide strips. Place rounded teaspoon peanut butter mixture about 1 inch from 1 end of each strip.

3. Starting at end of each strip with filling, fold corner of pastry dough over filling so it lines up with other side of strip, forming a triangle. Continue folding like a flag in triangular shape, using entire strip. Repeat process with remaining pastry dough and filling.

4. Place triangles about 2 inches apart on ungreased baking sheets, seam side down; spray with cooking spray. Bake 6 to 8 minutes or until golden brown. Remove from baking sheets to wire rack to cool.

5. Combine remaining 1 cup powdered sugar, 3 tablespoons syrup and water in small bowl. Glaze cookies just before serving.

Makes 28 cookies

Note: For longer storage, do not glaze cookies. Store loosely covered, so pastry dough remains crisp. Glaze before serving.

White Chocolate Truffles

1 ½ cups (10 ounces) chopped white chocolate or white chocolate chips
¼ cup whipping cream*
½ tablespoon vanilla
½ cup chopped macadamia nuts or toffee, or chocolate decors

*To flavor with liqueur, reduce cream to 2 tablespoons. Stir 2 tablespoons hazelnut- or almond-flavored liqueur into chocolate mixture along with vanilla.

1. Place chocolate in small bowl. Place whipping cream in small saucepan. Simmer over medium-high heat until heated through, stirring constantly with wooden spoon. Pour over chocolate; stir once.

2. Cover bowl; let stand 3 to 5 minutes. Uncover; stir until chocolate is melted and mixture is smooth. Stir in vanilla and liqueur, if using. Cover. Refrigerate 15 minutes or until mixture is firm enough to hold its shape.

3. Place level tablespoonfuls of mixture on plate; cover. Refrigerate 2 hours or until fudgy, but not soft.

4. Place nuts or toffee in medium bowl. Roll each tablespoon chocolate mixture into ball. Roll in nuts to evenly coat. (Warm hands and room temperature quickly soften chocolate, making it difficult to form balls. Keeping chocolate chilled prevents sticking.)

5. Serve chilled or let stand at room temperature 15 to 20 minutes before serving.

Smart Tip: Truffles that are in a tightly covered container can be refrigerated 2 to 3 days or frozen several weeks.

The publisher would like to thank the companies and organizations listed below for the use of their recipes and photographs in this publication.

A.1.® Steak Sauce
BelGioioso® Cheese, Inc.
Bestfoods
Birds Eye®
Butterball® Turkey Company
California Asparagus Commission
Campbell Soup Company
Chef Paul Prudhomme's Magic Seasoning Blends®
Del Monte Corporation
Dole Food Company, Inc.
Duncan Hines® and Moist Deluxe® are registered trademarks of Aurora Foods Inc.
Eagle® Brand
Egg Beaters®
Filippo Berio Olive Oil
Fleischmann's® Original Spread
Florida Department of Agriculture and Consumer Services, Bureau of Seafood and Aquaculture
Guiltless Gourmet®
Heinz U.S.A.
Hershey Foods Corporation
Hillshire Farm®
HONEY MAID® Honey Grahams
The HV Company
Idaho Potato Commission
Kahlúa® Liqueur
Kellogg Company
Kikkoman International Inc.

The Kingsford Products Company
KNOX® Unflavored Gelatine
Kraft Foods Holdings
Land O' Lakes, Inc.
Lawry's® Foods, Inc.
Lee Kum Kee (USA) Inc.
Lipton®
©Mars, Inc. 2000
National Cattlemen's Beef Association
National Fisheries Institute
National Honey Board
National Pork Producers Council
National Turkey Federation
Nestlé USA, Inc.
Perdue Farms Incorporated
PLANTERS® Nuts
The Procter & Gamble Company
Reckitt Benckiser
Riviana Foods Inc.
ROYAL® Desserts
Sargento® Foods Inc.
The J.M. Smucker Company
Southeast United Dairy Industry Association, Inc.
StarKist® Seafood Company
Uncle Ben's Inc.
Veg•All®
Walnut Marketing Board
Washington Apple Commission
Wisconsin Milk Marketing Board

VOLUME MEASUREMENTS (dry)

$1/8$ teaspoon = 0.5 mL
$1/4$ teaspoon = 1 mL
$1/2$ teaspoon = 2 mL
$3/4$ teaspoon = 4 mL
1 teaspoon = 5 mL
1 tablespoon = 15 mL
2 tablespoons = 30 mL
$1/4$ cup = 60 mL
$1/3$ cup = 75 mL
$1/2$ cup = 125 mL
$2/3$ cup = 150 mL
$3/4$ cup = 175 mL
1 cup = 250 mL
2 cups = 1 pint = 500 mL
3 cups = 750 mL
4 cups = 1 quart = 1 L

VOLUME MEASUREMENTS (fluid)

1 fluid ounce (2 tablespoons) = 30 mL
4 fluid ounces ($1/2$ cup) = 125 mL
8 fluid ounces (1 cup) = 250 mL
12 fluid ounces ($1 1/2$ cups) = 375 mL
16 fluid ounces (2 cups) = 500 mL

WEIGHTS (mass)

$1/2$ ounce = 15 g
1 ounce = 30 g
3 ounces = 90 g
4 ounces = 120 g
8 ounces = 225 g
10 ounces = 285 g
12 ounces = 360 g
16 ounces = 1 pound = 450 g

DIMENSIONS

$1/16$ inch = 2 mm
$1/8$ inch = 3 mm
$1/4$ inch = 6 mm
$1/2$ inch = 1.5 cm
$3/4$ inch = 2 cm
1 inch = 2.5 cm

OVEN TEMPERATURES

250°F = 120°C
275°F = 140°C
300°F = 150°C
325°F = 160°C
350°F = 180°C
375°F = 190°C
400°F = 200°C
425°F = 220°C
450°F = 230°C

BAKING PAN SIZES

Utensil	Size in Inches/Quarts	Metric Volume	Size in Centimeters
Baking or Cake Pan (square or rectangular)	8×8×2	2 L	20×20×5
	9×9×2	2.5 L	23×23×5
	12×8×2	3 L	30×20×5
	13×9×2	3.5 L	33×23×5
Loaf Pan	8×4×3	1.5 L	20×10×7
	9×5×3	2 L	23×13×7
Round Layer Cake Pan	8×1½	1.2 L	20×4
	9×1½	1.5 L	23×4
Pie Plate	8×1¼	750 mL	20×3
	9×1¼	1 L	23×3
Baking Dish or Casserole	1 quart	1 L	—
	1½ quart	1.5 L	—
	2 quart	2 L	—